The
Reference
Shelf

Volunteerism

Edited by Frank McGuckin

The Reference Shelf
Volume 70 • Number 4

The H. W. Wilson Company
New York • Dublin
1998

The Reference Shelf

The books in this series contain reprints of articles, excerpts from books, addresses on current issues, and studies of social trends in the United States and other countries. There are six separately bound numbers in each volume, all of which are usually published in the same calendar year. Numbers one through five are each devoted to a single subject, providing background information and discussion from various points of view and concluding with a subject index and comprehensive bibliography that lists books, pamphlets, and abstracts of additional articles on the subject. The final number of each volume is a collection of recent speeches, and it contains a cumulative speaker index. Books may be purchased individually or on subscription.

Visit H. W. Wilson's web site: http://www.hwwilson.com

Library of Congress Cataloging-in-Publication Data

Volunteerism/edited by Frank McGuckin.
      p. cm.—(The reference shelf; v. 70, no. 4)
    Includes bibliographical references and index.
    ISBN 0-8242-0944-3
    1. Voluntarism—United States.   I. McGuckin, Frank, 1971–
  II. Series.
HN79.V63V65 1998   98-35206
361.3'7'0973—dc21   CIP

Cover: A volunteer sweeps up debris at a park.
Photo: AP/Wide World Photos

Printed in the United States of America

Contents

Preface

"Ask not what your country can do for you—ask what you can do for your country," said President John F. Kennedy during his inaugural address on January 20, 1961, taking the initiative and attempting to tackle the difficult problems facing the nation. The response to his speech was overwhelming; among those who answered his call were not only volunteers for the Peace Corps, created two months later, and Volunteers in Service to America (VISTA), created in the mid-1960s, but also those who joined the military and those who took their professional training in education, law, and medicine to the inner cities. Kennedy's challenge affected the spirit of the nation and established an enduring volunteer culture that has touched the lives of millions. Today, nearly 20,000 people donate blood to the Red Cross every day— enough for up to 80,000 lifesaving transfusions—and billions of pounds of surplus food are distributed to starving people every year. A child mentored by a Big Brother or Big Sister is 46 percent less likely to use drugs and 33 percent less likely to hit someone. Volunteers save lives.

While preparing to enter a new century, many citizens are concerned about difficult national problems—our economic, social, political, and domestic problems, especially the homeless and poor. Children have a harder times these days becoming successful when pessimism and negativity fill a society. According to some experts, education should be the most important element of social progress. Supporting this was the generation of young people in America during the 1960s that responded to President Kennedy. National services such as the Peace Corps, VISTA, and AmeriCorps are established programs that not only help, but also teach. Under the leadership of President Bill Clinton, Congress passed the National and Community Service Trust Act of 1993, which reinstated some civic responsibility in the United States and called upon citizens to serve in programs that will benefit the nation by improving opportunities for the young. Younger and older Americans want to be involved in activities that help others and would not otherwise be performed by career-oriented people. Every generation responds to President Kennedy's challenge in its own way and recent events dictate that an important part of this generation's response will be community service—voluntary involvement in dealing directly and personally with others. People want to make a difference; they want to help and be asked for help by others, and to be respected for it.

Volunteers have been involved with the public since the days of town meetings. Many were elected to serve on policy-making and school boards, and many others were elected or appointed to commissions. Section I, Society's Responsibility and Commitment, provides an outlook on recent volunteer activity and what can be done about the problems of the poor, the elderly, the handicapped, and other disadvantaged groups in the population; this section also examines efforts to construct a basis for action on behalf of such groups. The articles in this section demonstrate that new volunteer projects can be created that fit easily into busy schedules and require only a short-term commitment. Even for those who already have a job, there are still ways to find something that allows them to participate and provides interest for the individuals.

Since the mid-1900s, local citizen participation in federally financed government programs has been mandated by law for both decision-making and service roles of a particular project. Voluntary organizations, regardless of size, have a dual responsibility: to provide a service and to enhance the sense of community. Section II, Private Volunteering and AmeriCorps, explores a sample of groups in various types of communities that depend on the joint efforts of people to achieve their collective goals. Two articles critique AmeriCorps, which embodies the federal government's involvement in efforts to volunteer. Some critics have suggested that these groups are "using" volunteers or "requiring the unpaid work" of volunteers primarily because of budget or personnel limitations. But others have contended that increased efficiency is only one reason for relying on volunteers. When social agencies, for example, work with volunteers, it is not merely to add manpower, but also to strengthen the sense of responsibility that we all have for each other; also important to our democracy is an understanding of our responsibilities as well as our rights. The voluntary organization is a channel through which the dignity of the individual can be developed, and through which his or her rights and responsibilities can be exercised on matters pertaining to social policy.

Volunteers can fill some of the gaps in the social net, but probably not all of them. Ninety-three million Americans volunteer according to the Independent Sector. They contributed over 20 billion hours in 1995. Section III, Volunteerism Is Not Enough, takes a closer look at those figures and raises some questions. Many volunteer hours are spent on informal volunteering, like babysitting or participating in church fundraisers, and many volunteers donate their time to private school functions or local shops. Other volunteers serve as tutors or mentors. A large portion of volunteer work is done for local churches, which is certainly valuable, but only a small proportion of it serves the community directly. Volunteer efforts also have the potential to be poorly organized and managed.

Volunteer work *can* help repair failing communities. Many advocates believe that the only way to get people involved in their communities is to teach them how; others argue that community involvement requires time off from work. Major companies have given such opportunities to their workers. Even without that incentive, people are willing to help others as demonstrated during the recent floods in North Dakota or the fires in Florida, when Americans turned out in droves to help the victims. Section IV, Rewards of Volunteerism, describes different ways that volunteers gain satisfaction from the good that they do. In particular, people who make the sustained, years-long commitment to serve as mentors to poor or troubled kids deserve praise. Such efforts combine empathy and practicality, both worthy traits, and the nation is full of kids who need a reason to be hopeful. Every weekend, Americans do important, meaningful work without benefit of politicians or TV cameras. Volunteerism preserves and transmits the value of compassion by giving adults and children a chance to help themselves as well as the great many of those in need across the world. For most volunteers, sharing their time and effort gives them a sense of purpose and an opportunity to serve their nation.

The editor would like to thank all the authors and publishers who responded and granted permission to reprint the material contained in this issue of the Reference Shelf. The editor would also like to express great appreciation to Michael Schulze, director of General Reference, Hilary Claggett, senior editor, Beth Levy, associate editor, and Irene Astorga, assistant art director. Special thanks to all those who "volunteered" their services, especially to Mark Rupprecht and Ron Giammarco for "volunteering" their time.

Frank McGuckin
July 1998

I. Society's Responsibility and Commitment

Editor's Introduction

Volunteerism is recognizing that a need exists and responding to that need out of one's own initiative; it is not an act following a certain mandate dictated by an authority. In response to the needs of society, volunteers give not only material things but also service, time, and energy. The services are rendered without payment, and the volunteers work in partnership with an organization or institution. The volunteer movement in the United States has continued to grow and expand, and it is still characterized by many of the same features upon which it was created. Section I examines the ongoing changes and needs of volunteerism and the role of the volunteer as well as his or her impact on the American way of life.

If volunteerism yields so many benefits, one might ask, why aren't more people volunteering? Some have suggested that not enough people know how to put their pride aside and illuminate all the "right" reasons to be a positive force in promoting volunteerism. In a speech delivered to the Recognition Banquet at Wayland Baptist University, Benjamin Akande weighs prosperity versus social responsibility. He discusses the prospects of missing a chance to make a difference. His speech evaluates the value of giving back to society and the commitment to make a difference. Akande comments on the Retired & Senior Volunteer Program (RSVP) as a powerful force that contributes to the general welfare.

Some senior citizens are taking the prospect of social responsibility a little further by not waiting to be called upon to take action. In an article from *USA Today*, Marc Freedman explains that many retirees want to use their years of experience in a wide variety of programs. This movement has a great chance for success since the population of retirees in America is growing rapidly. The author also gives an outline of senior citizens' strong points, providing a valuable perspective on the limitations and future direction that volunteerism can take with their assistance.

Service-learning and volunteerism are significant means through which higher education can reach some of its most far-reaching goals, including its own commitment to service. A book excerpt taken from *Service-Learning in Higher Education: Concepts and Practices*, by Barbara Jacoby, defines service-learning as a "form of experiential education in which students engage in activities that address human and community needs together with structured opportunities intentionally designed to promote student learning and development." Furthermore, she argues that service-learning is both "curricular and cocurricular, because all learning does not occur in the classroom," and that it can yield a "wide range of outcomes," especially community enhancement. From a collegiate level, educators can promote student learning, strengthen teaching and research, and pull together many resources to meet society's problems and needs.

The editors of the *Ladies' Home Journal*, in conjunction with the Points of Light Foundation, have launched a community-service campaign of their own called the Millennium Project. In an article from the *Ladies' Home Journal*, Lynn Harris profiles dedicated individuals involved in this program. Inspired by the recent summit on volof prosperity if there are so many good people weighed down by the burdens of life? What is the significance of having so much if we allow those that have so little to go untouched? What is prosperity if we can't enrich our community by dedicating ourselves to a cause that is greater than ourselves?

Prosperity is not about how successful we are or how successful we can be. Prosperity is about how we can make others around us better. Prosperity is about fulfillment, responsibility and commitment to our community. Prosperity is about being our brother's and our sister's keeper. Believe me, prosperity is a powerful tool, and if used properly, it can create a better society. If you are searching for the meaning of prosperity, if you are looking for a true demonstration of prosperity, you need not look any further. You can find it in the Retired Seniors Volunteer Program. RSVP provides the avenue to share our prosperity.

"Real prosperity is measured...in the sacred notion of giving back to society."

I must submit to you tonight that the prosperity of which I speak cannot be measured by wealth, nor can it be measured by income. In my opinion, real prosperity is measured in the demonstration in the value of sharing, in the sacred notion of giving back to society and in the commitment to make a difference. This is the uniqueness of RSVP. I would like to commend every volunteer in this room tonight. It is these volunteers that have demonstrated beyond reproach, the power of giving and the power of lending a helping hand.

We live in a society in which so many of us allow stumbling blocks, societal hurdles, impossibilities. It's never been done before, to discourage us from doing the right thing. In my opinion, RSVP has turned stumbling blocks into stepping stones.

I am reminded of a story of four people that many of you may know. Their names are: everybody, somebody, anybody and nobody. These four people had a job to do and everybody was asked to do it. But everybody was sure that somebody would do it, anybody could have done it, but nobody did it. Somebody got angry because it was everybody's job. Everybody thought anybody could do it, but nobody realized that everybody wouldn't do it. It ended up that everybody blamed somebody when nobody did what anybody could have done.

Life is a bus load full of people on a journey. Where we are going and how and when we reach our final destination, depends on the collective effort of the drivers as well as the passengers. In this journey of life for which we all must take but once, we are all on this bus; we are the drivers, we are the passengers. And so, tonight we make a brief stop on this journey. We pause to refuel our conscience, to strengthen our resolve. Tonight we are here to rededicate ourselves, to recommit ourselves to the task of building our community.

The good people at RSVP are a living testimony that we can do more together than we can apart. They remind us that no matter what talents an individual possesses, no matter the energy an individual may have, one individual can accomplish very little, but when we are sustained by a group of people, who are dedicated to the same cause, when there is shared vision and resolve, we can accomplish a great deal. In fact, we can accomplish anything.

I leave you this evening having found the answer to the question: What is the meaning of prosperity? Prosperity gives us significance, it gives us purpose and meaning. I have found the meaning of prosperity, in the people and in the work of RSVP. RSVP gives meaning to our lives. RSVP has demonstrated that it is up to me and you to make a difference. I'm reminded of a prayer of Saint Francis of Assisi:

> Lord make me an instrument of your peace.
> Where there is hatred, let me sow love.
> Where there is injury, pardon.
> Where there is doubt, faith.
> Where there is despair, hope.
> Where there is darkness, light.
> Where there is sadness, joy.
> Divine Master, grant that I may not so much seek
> To be consoled, but to console;
> To be understood, as to understand:
> To be loved, as to love;
> For it is in giving that we receive.

Oliver Wendell Holmes Jr. reminds us that to find the great things in this life, it is not so much where we stand as in what direction we are moving. RSVP is moving Plainview in the right direction.

I have found the meaning of prosperity, and if you are looking for it, you too will find it. You will find it in the 691 volunteers who have labored for 120,312 hours. You can find it in the hearts, and minds, and in the deeds of the volunteers of RSVP. You can find it in this room tonight. May the Lord continue to strengthen you and watch over you all the days of your life. Thank you and God bless you.

Senior Citizens: A New Force in Community Service[2]

With retirees living longer and generally enjoying better health, many are seeking ways to provide their experience and expertise in a wide range of programs.

"Many older Americans are in a position to make the major life commitment...that defines national service."

As the baby boom generation approaches retirement and life expectancy continues to increase, the U.S. finds itself in the midst of a demographic revolution. The senior population is twice what it was in 1960 and is expected to double again over the next 30 years. By the middle of the 21st century, seniors will out-number children and youth for the first time. Few other changes are likely to exert as great an influence on society in the coming decades.

For the most part, the aging of American society is portrayed as a source of impending strife, with new strains on families, social services, and inter-generational relations. While this transformation presents real challenges, it brings new opportunities as well. The U.S. today possesses not only the fastest growing, but the largest, best-educated, and most vigorous collection of older adults in its history. In fact, the senior population may represent the country's sole increasing natural resource.

How might the productive and humanitarian potential of this resource be harnessed at a juncture when unmet needs in education, health care, public safety, the environment, and other essential areas are extensive and urgent? National service offers a particularly appealing vehicle for engaging seniors to respond to pressing needs. Many older Americans are in a position to make the major life commitment—ranging from half- to full-time work for at least one year—that defines national service.

The rationale for senior participation in national service centers on three overlapping and complementary objectives: alleviating the country's pressing domestic problems; enhancing the personal development of participants; and bolstering the nation's flagging sense of community.

In the context of America's considerable unmet needs, seniors represent hope not only because they are numerous, but because they are potentially available. Increased longevity and early retirement means they are spending a greater proportion of their lives in post-retirement—for many, one-third of their lives. Studies show that retirement frees substantial amounts of time—an average of 25 hours per week for men and 18 hours for women—and that most is spent either watching television or

---

[2] Article by Marc Freedman, Director of Special Projects, Public/Private Ventures, Philadelphia, PA, from *USA Today* 125:54-7 Ja '97. Copyright © 1997 *USA Today.* Reprinted with permission.

doing housework.

There also are indications that older adults are looking for opportunities to serve. A study sponsored by the U.S. Administration on Aging found that 14,000,000 Americans over the age of 65 (37.4% of the senior population) might be willing to come forward if asked, while 4,000,000 current volunteers indicate they would like to give more time. Forty percent of those surveyed say the government should be doing more to promote service opportunities.

Older adults may be particularly appropriate for national service assignments. They are experienced workers, family members, and citizens, among other things, and therefore are a rich repository of the social capital required by young people to make the transition to adulthood. Studies of older workers and volunteers further suggest that seniors bring reliability, dependability, and discipline to responsible assignments.

For many, retirement means a jarring transition from engagement to disengagement, from productivity to idleness. Fifty-five percent of elder respondents to a Louis Harris Poll lamented the loss of usefulness after retirement. Isolation and lack of purpose have been shown to increase seniors' risk of deterioration, illness, and death. Conversely, productive engagement and strong social networks contribute to prolonged mental and physical health. A 25-year National Institute of Mental Health study found, for example, that "highly organized" activity is the single strongest predictor, other than not smoking, of longevity and vitality.

Service provides opportunities for engagement, activity, acquaintanceship, and growth. According to sociologist Erik Erikson, service can meet a deeper need as well, satisfying the impulse toward generativity—the instinctual drive to pass on to the next generation what an individual has learned from life. The final challenge of life, he maintains, involves coming to terms with the notion, "I am what survives of me."

In the 1980s, Americans began hearing about the prospect of coming generational conflict, sparked by the contention that seniors were depriving the country's children and youth of their fair share in a political process dominated by elder interests. This argument usually is overstated, but there can be no doubt that, in a society divided by class, race, and sex, tensions between the generations exist as well. In the absence of cross-generational contact and engagement, these tensions might worsen as the demographic composition of society continues to shift.

National service for seniors—particularly intergenerational efforts—provide a potential antidote to these tensions. Indeed, there is evidence suggesting just such an effect. In the early 1980s, for instance, Miami aggressively began pursuing elder school volunteers, who then became the linchpin in a campaign for passage of a billion-dollar school bond issue.

Engaging seniors through service can contribute to preserving the essential features of civil society, which, many have concluded, is unraveling. In this context, the idea of senior service is compelling, in the words of anthropologist Margaret Mead, "as a way to restore a sense of community, a knowledge of the past, and a sense of the future."

While compelling in the abstract, the idea of senior service by no means is an untested notion. Beginning three decades ago and proceeding in fits and starts, a partial system of national service for seniors has developed in this country. This experience offers rich lessons for policy and programs.

In spring, 1963, Pres. John F. Kennedy delivered his most important speech on aging, decrying the "wall of inertia" standing between old people and their communities. In response, Kennedy urged the establishment of a National Service Corps, a domestic equivalent of the Peace Corps, that would provide opportunities for community service involving both the elderly and the young. The President's call was an invitation, in Attorney General Robert F. Kennedy's words, to "millions of older and retired people whose reservoir of skill and experience remains untapped."

"These programs engage 100,000 older Americans in year-round...community service."

The National Service Corps proposal to engage a wide swath of older Americans never made it out of Congress, and with its demise went an encompassing vision of senior participation in national service that remains unfulfilled today. In 1965, however, a more limited incarnation of senior service emerged when Pres. Lyndon Johnson announced Federal funding for a new set of programs engaging low-income seniors in community service. The most prominent new efforts were the Foster Grandparent and Green Thumb programs, both administered originally by the Office of Economic Opportunity (OEO) and paying participating seniors stipends equivalent to the minimum wage. Foster Grandparents paired seniors one-to-one with children and youth who were disadvantaged or disabled, while Green Thumb, sponsored by the National Farmers Union, engaged older adults in highway beautification and other community service projects.

Over time, the Foster Grandparent Program moved to the Department of Health, Education and Welfare, eventually becoming part of the Federal volunteer service agency ACTION in 1971. Green Thumb, meanwhile, moved from OEO to Department of Labor jurisdiction and, in the process, developed greater emphasis on public service employment and job placement. It was joined by projects administered by the National Council on the Aging, National Council of Senior Citizens, American Association of Retired Persons, and other leading organizations—all of which eventually became the Senior Community Service Employment Program, Title V of the Older Americans Act. In 1973, the Senior Companion Program, based on a model similar to Foster Grandparents and also lodged in ACTION, was started to provide one-to-one support to frail elders.

Today, these programs engage 100,000 older Americans in year-round, intensive, stipended community service of 20 hours per week. While other Federally funded initiatives, such as the Peace Corps, VISTA, and RSVP, involve older adults in projects requiring the commitment associated with service, the overwhelming majority of current opportunities are concentrated in the Foster Grandparent, Senior Companion, and Title V initiatives.

Lessons from Experience

Examining the experience of established and incipient efforts provides a valuable perspective on the promise, limitations, and future directions for national and community service involving seniors.

- Seniors can provide essential community service. Evidence of the important contribution of seniors in Federally funded service programs is chronicled in more than 70 studies over 30 years. The vast majority of this research, focused on the Foster Grandparent and Senior Companion programs, suggests substantial benefits both to individual clients and host agencies, indicating that seniors fill significant service gaps, provide complementary skills to staff and other volunteers, and are stable and long-lasting participants.

- Seniors can benefit through serving. The motive driving senior service appears to be less altruism than a strong and straightforward desire for structure, purpose, affiliation, growth, and meaning. There is evidence from program evaluations and other research suggesting that older participants derive these benefits from the service experience. One study finds, for instance, that participants experience "increased self-esteem, renewed feelings of health and vigor, and new and satisfying social relationships with peers."

- Low-income seniors can play an important role in service. The vast majority of existing service programs enroll low-income seniors, most of them women and many minorities. The efforts of the past three decades demonstrate that these low-income individuals—the group most likely to be overlooked and undervalued for their assets—can make a substantial contribution to their communities and can benefit in the process.

- Government can enable senior service. The current roster of service programs operates on a national scale, involving more than 1,000 projects and 100,000 participants. They demonstrate the important enabling role government can play in the service arena by stimulating, supporting, and sustaining service efforts through providing ongoing infrastructure, and doing so without suffocating civic spirit or compromising local control. The experience of these programs also highlights their political resilience. They have navigated seven administrations, Democratic and Republican, while building bipartisan support along the way.

- Implementation is crucial. Effective senior service requires sturdy infrastructure not only at the policy level—as reflected in the government's ongoing enabling role—but at the program level as well. An overarching lesson of the past three decades' experience in this arena is that program implementation is essential. Experience to date provides increased sophistication in this arena and a set of lessons concerning the best program practices for training, recruitment, compensation, and supervision.

- Senior service is not cheap. It is not practical simply to call for participants, parcel them out, and hope for the best. Responsible programming costs money, notably for adequate staffing and supervision. At present, the annual Federal cost for the Foster Grandparent Program is $65,800,000 ($3,508 per slot); the Senior Companion Program, $29,000,000 ($3,723 a slot); and the Senior Community Service Employment Program, $390,000,000 ($6,053 per slot). The lower cost per slot of the first two programs is attributable primarily to differences in compensation. The Foster Grandparent and Senior Companion programs pay a tax-exempt stipend of $2.45 per hour, while the Senior Community Service Employment Program provides taxable compensation pegged to the minimum wage.

- Critical mass is missing. While the absolute numbers involved in senior community service are impressive, these efforts remain small, scarce, and scattered at the ground level. Only about one-quarter of one percent of seniors are involved nationally, in contrast to the roughly five percent of the eligible population engaged in the Depression-era Civilian Conservation Corps. The Foster Grandparent and Senior Companion programs are available in just a small fraction of the counties and have long waiting lists of interested participants.

- Program limitations exist. First, very few men participate in the programs—11% of Foster Grandparents, 15% of Senior Companions, and 34% in the Senior Community Service Employment Program are male. Second, by law, these efforts are restricted to low-income individuals, screening out many working- and middle-class seniors—including large numbers on fixed incomes that still put them slightly above the eligibility line. Third, available assignments tend to be caregiving, delivering Meals on Wheels, or providing support services—offerings that do not begin to approximate the wider variety of tasks seniors might contribute.

- Obstacles and questions remain. Despite progress, a cultural ambivalence about older adults as serious, capable, and productive citizens and service-providers persists. At the organizational level, underutilization of seniors in service assignments is a serious problem, ranging from being ignored through being placed in assignments that do not make full use of their skills and abilities. Host agency personnel often are overwhelmed with other duties, lack training in working with seniors in service roles, or are concerned that elders will impinge on their turf or even displace regular staff. Indeed, knowledge is lacking about many key issues related to senior service, including displacement and cost-effectiveness. Over the past 30 years, a great deal has been accomplished in senior service, constructing the rudiments of a national service system for older Americans and developing an understanding about what it takes to put senior service into action. These accomplishments notwithstanding, the gap between promise and practice remains substantial.

"A central task is to close the senior service gap."

In many ways, the nation still is subsisting on innovations dating back to the War on Poverty. The great triumph of this legacy is the involvement of low-income seniors in essential community service; the great limitation can be found in the absence of opportunities for the vast remainder of the senior population.

Today, with national service in the public mind, there is an opportunity to re-examine this legacy, to build on the achievements of the 1960s while preparing for the circumstances of the 2020s. A central task is to close the senior service gap, not only out of a desire to meet current needs, but to produce what historian Peter Laslett calls an "institutional inheritance" for the coming wave of older Americans.

In moving forward, an effort should be made to engage a wider range of older adults (in terms of education, income, and sex), provide an expanded menu of service roles (within existing programs and through new opportunities), and create mechanisms for meeting essential community needs while stimulating the growth and development of participants. A system should be created that provides opportunities at a variety of levels—not merely the chance to volunteer a few hours a week (where immense progress has been made over the past generation), but to serve in well-developed half- and full-time opportunities. If these efforts were linked effectively, interested seniors might be in the position to move in and out of various options, perhaps serving half time or more for a year or two, then making the transition to assignments requiring a less encompassing commitment.

Throughout, these efforts should be anchored in a vision of senior service that is substantially, though not exclusively, intergenerational, involving not only opportunities for seniors to serve the younger generation, but to serve side by side with youth for the good of the community. A reasonable goal for these efforts would be creation of high-impact, well-crafted senior service opportunities for one percent of the senior population, or approximately 500,000 adults 65 years and older, by 2020. The Federal cost for this undertaking would be about $3,000,000,000 in current dollars (at an average per-senior cost of $6,000 for half-time service, a figure reflecting additional investment in strengthening program practices). In return, communities would receive 500,000,000 hours of annual elder service.

Strategic Planning

An incremental strategy in pursuing this objective is prudent. Current slots should be expanded from 100,000 to 150,000 over the next five years, then steadily built toward one percent of the population, and that proportion maintained as the older adult cohort increases in size. Achieving this vision for senior service in America will require progress on the following fronts:

Strengthen the three programs currently providing the vast majority of senior service opportunities. First, expand the Foster Grandparent and Senior Companion Programs. Five years after the Foster Grandparent Program was created, the Senate Special Committee on Aging, citing the program's record of achievement, called for an increase in its size to 60,000. A quarter-century later, the initiative barely is one-third this size, and the Foster Grandparent and Senior Companion programs combined enroll just over half this number. Meanwhile, the vast need for caregiving for children and youth on one hand, and older adults and the ailing on the other—as well as the track record of these programs—strongly support dramatic expansion.

Second, re-examine the service dimension of the Senior Community Service Employment Program. Much effort over the past decade has been spent fortifying its job transition aspect. Interviews with participants, program operators, and national officials suggest that the community service component of Title V might benefit from revamping. Currently, at least two informal strands exist within this program. One primarily serves younger enrollees who join for help in returning to unsubsidized jobs. The second, much larger strand serves "career enrollees," those who essentially have stopped looking for unsubsidized work and most likely will remain in subsidized community service placements in nonprofit and public agencies for substantial periods. This second strand should be bolstered to raise the priority, quality, and level of service performed, enabling participants to provide the greatest possible contribution to their communities.

Embark on a period of innovation and experimentation. Engage male seniors, a group that has been reluctant to participate in existing efforts. In addition to making the Foster Grandparent and Senior Companion programs more attractive to this group, establishing new program areas such as environmental work, apprenticeship efforts, and professional services might draw a greater proportion of men.

Secure the participation of seniors living above poverty circumstances. A variety of routes toward this goal might be pursued. For example, a portion of expanded Foster Grandparent and Senior Companion slots might be freed from income guidelines entirely. Another option is to develop a high-intensity, stipended, half- to full-time track within the Retired and Senior Volunteer Program, which currently is open to participation regardless of income, but is oriented toward assignments involving two to four hours of uncompensated voluntarism a week.

Develop intergenerational programs in which seniors and youth serve jointly. It is necessary to explore partnerships, for instance, between senior service and youth service efforts, including opportunities for seniors and youth to serve side by side in the new AmeriCorps initiative. The concept of an intergenerational service corps equally balanced between senior and youth participants should be explored.

Conduct experiments involving a variety of compensation and program strategies. It would be useful to compare, for example, the different effects of tax-exempt, sub-minimum wage stipends and taxable stipends at the minimum-wage level and higher. Alternative forms of compensation such as service credits, health benefits, long-term care credits, or even property tax relief might be explored, along with a variety of strategies in such areas as training, supervision, and support.

Build infrastructure at the national and local levels. Establish a national center for senior service. A new entity is needed capable of providing muscle to a set of essential—and long-neglected—marketing, technical assistance, demonstration, and research functions designed to raise the level of knowledge, awareness, and implementation of senior service across the country. While some of these functions might be carried out internally by the Corporation for National and Community Service, the creation of a not-for-profit intermediary organization probably is preferable. This institution should be established through collaboration by the Corporation and private sponsors, including foundations and major organizations for the aging.

Create mechanisms at the local level to give visibility and meaning to the senior corps concept. Such local mechanisms, which well might evolve out of existing structures, would act as a single point of entry for older adults; perform local marketing among seniors and others in the community; conduct training for seniors involved in community service; develop the capacity of community agencies to use the talents of seniors; promulgate new initiatives designed to meet local needs; and provide opportunities for contact among elders participating in different programs.

Moving forward with this agenda promises potential benefits not only to recipients of service and participating seniors, but to society at large. Anchored on sturdy institutional moorings, senior service might help to create a more generative society, dedicated to posterity, striving to extend Erik Erikson's "I am what survives of me" until it becomes the defining outlook of a generation.

Service-Learning in Today's Higher Education[3]

Higher education is being called on to renew its historic commitment to service. Its foremost experts are urging colleges and universities to assume a leadership role in addressing society's increasing problems and in meeting growing human needs. Indeed, their calls to action serve as a collective mandate for higher education to become actively engaged in responding to these problems and needs. Ernest Boyer urges colleges and universities to "respond to the challenges that confront our children, our schools, and our cities, just as the land-grant colleges responded to the needs of agriculture and industry a century ago." Derek Bok agrees: "There is no reason for universities to feel uncomfortable in taking account of society's needs; in fact, they have a clear obligation to do so." A renewed commitment to service will go a long way in responding to higher education's critics who bemoan its "fortress mentality" in isolating itself from the encroaching problems of both its local communities and the rest of the nation.

"There is no reason for universities to feel uncomfortable in taking account of society's needs."

At the same time, higher education is questioning its effectiveness at achieving its most fundamental goal: student learning. Numerous articles and reports have criticized indifferent undergraduate teaching, overemphasis on esoteric research, failure to promote moral character and civic consciousness, and narrow focus on preparing graduates for the job market.

Today's college students, however, feeling compelled to confront society's problems, are participating in community service in record numbers. In Alexander Astin's research on a sample of students who entered college in the fall of 1994, more than 70 percent reported that they had performed volunteer work in high school. As more and more elementary and secondary schools are requiring community service, this percentage will only increase.

Indeed, Arthur Levine's 1993 survey of nine thousand undergraduates reveals that 64 percent were involved in volunteer activities. This involvement occurs at all types of institutions of higher education: community colleges (59 percent), four-year colleges (67 percent), and universities (68 percent). Both men (62 percent) and women (66 percent) are involved, as are both older (63 percent) and younger (65 percent) students. The percentages are high for white students (65 percent), as well as for students of color (62 percent). And the trend is established in all regions of the country: the Northeast (61 percent), the Midwest (65 percent), then South (64 percent), and the West (67 percent).

---

[3] Book excerpt by Barbara Jacoby, director of the Office of Commuter Affairs and Community Service Programs at the University of Maryland at College Park and author of *The Student as Commuter: Developing a Comprehensive Institutional Response* (1989), from *Service-Learning in Higher Education.* Copyright © 1996 Jossey-Bass Inc., Publishers. Reprinted with permission.

Students participate in a wide range of community service activities, working with children, teenagers, people with physical and mental disabilities, people who are elderly, battered women, and people with AIDS. Their work addresses issues of hunger, homelessness, illiteracy, health care, educational disadvantage, the environment, and numerous others. Robert Coles, the well-respected Harvard service-learning educator, points out that in contrast to the young people of the 1960s, "today's students are likely to express their lofty political and social impulses and practical desires to change the world through community service."

As colleges and universities across the country are developing programs to enable their students to serve their communities, the nation, and the world—and at the same time to enrich under graduate education—it is critical that these programs embrace the concept of service-learning. This chapter defines service-learning and elucidates the differences between service-learning and traditional community service. It provides a historical overview and a context for understanding the essential linkage of service and learning; it describes the current state of practice; and it highlights the relationship between service-learning and institutional educational goals.

Service-Learning Defined

Robert Sigmon notes that "many definitions and approaches have been used within the general framework of linking service with learning." In the introduction to *Combining Service and Learning* (1990), Jane Kendall states that she participated in hundreds of debates about the language used in combining service and learning, "debates that will probably rage forever." She adds that she encountered 147 terms in the literature she reviewed; even more are in use today.

For the purposes of this book, service-learning is defined as follows:

> Service-learning is a form of experiential education in which students engage in activities that address human and community needs together with structured opportunities intentionally designed to promote student learning and development. Reflection and reciprocity are key concepts of service-learning.

The hyphen in *service-learning* is critical in that it symbolizes the symbiotic relationship between service and learning. The term *community* in the definition of service-learning refers to local neighborhoods, the state, the nation, and the global community. The human and community needs that service-learning addresses are those needs that are *defined by the community*.

Sigmon proposes a useful service and learning typology with four variations found at colleges and universities: "service-LEARNING," which implies that learning goals are primary and service outcomes secondary; "SERVICE-learning," in which the service agenda is central and the learning secondary; "service learning," in which the absence of the hyphen indicates that the two are viewed as completely separate from each other; and SERVICE-LEARNING," in which service and learning goals are of equal weight and "the hyphen is essential." This last relationship, which Sigmon prefers, is advocated in this book.

This book takes the firm stance that service-learning is both curricular and cocurricular, because all learning does not occur in the classroom. Although some current definitions of service-learning insist that it must be integrated into the curriculum, student learning is indeed structured and facilitated by student affairs professionals, campus ministers, trained student leaders, and community members in addition to faculty. Although the structure afforded by the curriculum (class meetings, syllabi, assignments, grading, and credit) makes it easier to hold students accountable for achieving the desired outcomes of service-learning, skillfully designed and implemented cocurricular experiences can yield rich results. And learning and developmental outcomes are not necessarily related to a discipline or to particular course content....

"The work of theorists and researchers on learning... indicates that we learn through combinations of thought and action."

Discussion also continues about whether one-time or short-term experiences, such as serving in a soup kitchen or participating in an environmental cleanup project, can be called service-learning. This book posits that they can if they include the fundamental concepts of reflection and reciprocity, which distinguish service-learning from other community service and volunteer programs. Some of these programs include some elements of these concepts, but many do not. The use of the term *service-learning* implies the centrality of reflection and reciprocity to both conception and practice.

Reflection

As a form of experiential education, service-learning is based on the pedagogical principle that learning and development do not necessarily occur as a result of experience itself but as a result of a reflective component explicitly designed to foster learning and development. The work of theorists and researchers on learning—from Jean Piaget to William Perry, from James Coleman to David Kolb, from John Dewey to Donald Schon—indicates that we learn through combinations of thought and action, reflection and practice, theory and application. Different service-learning programs emphasize different types of learning goals: intellectual, civic, ethical, moral, cross-cultural, career, or personal. Programs also highlight different combinations of these goals.

Service-learning programs are also explicitly structured to promote learning about the larger social issues behind the needs to which their service is responding. This learning includes a deeper understanding of the historical, sociological, cultural, economic, and political contexts of the needs or issues being addressed. Reflection could be designed, for example, to encourage students working in a homeless shelter to ask such questions as Why are there homeless people? What national and state policies affect homelessness? Why do we create homeless shelters rather than identify and solve the root causes of the problem? If homelessness is a global problem, how do other countries deal with it? Reflection can take many forms: individual and group, oral and written, directly related to discipline-based course material or not. Reflection should include opportunities for participants to receive feedback from those persons being served, as well as from peers and program leaders.

Reciprocity

The other essential concept of service-learning is reciprocity between the server and the person or group being served. "All parties in service-learning are learners and help determine what is to be learned. Both the server and those served teach, and both learn." In service-learning, those being served control the service provided. The needs of the community, as determined by its members, define what the service tasks will be. Service-learning avoids placing students into community settings based solely on desired student learning outcomes and providing services that do not meet actual needs or perpetuate a state of need rather than seeking and addressing the causes of need.

Through reciprocity, students develop a greater sense of belonging and responsibility as members of a larger community. Community members being served learn how to take responsibility for their own needs and become empowered to develop mechanisms and relationships to address them. Thus, reciprocity creates "a sense of mutual responsibility and respect between individuals in the service-learning exchange." Service-learning thus stands in contrast to the traditional, paternalistic, one-way approach to service, where one person or group has resources that they share with a person or group that they assume lacks resources. Reciprocity also eschews the traditional concept of volunteerism, which is based on the idea that a more competent person comes to the aid of a less competent person. In the old paradigm, volunteers often attempt to solve other people's problems before fully understanding the situation or its causes. Service-learning encourages students to do things *with* others rather than *for* them. Everyone should expect to change in the process.

Some authors have legitimately challenged the use of the word *service* in service-learning. They point out that it suggests inequality among the participants in service-learning, with an individual or group doing something to another individual or group. It goes against the "parity of esteem," as Howard Berry terms the mutuality of the service-learning exchange. For many African Americans and other people who have experienced oppression, *service* still connotes involuntary servitude. *Service* is also used in a self-righteous sense to mean well-endowed persons "doing things" for those who are less fortunate than themselves. Nevertheless, I agree with Kendall and Berry that although the word *service* is problematic, it is the most common and accessible word to use.

Service-Learning as Program, Philosophy, and Pedagogy

In this book, and in numerous other contexts, service-learning is often referred to as a program. Although it is convenient to speak of service-learning programs in higher education, it is important to note here that service-learning is also a philosophy and a pedagogy; unfortunately, it is sometimes construed as a political stance. As a program, service-learning emphasizes the accomplishment of tasks to meet human and community needs in combination with "intentional learning goals and with conscious reflection and critical analysis." Tasks in which participants engage are often direct services, such as tutoring, work in soup kitchens and homeless shelters, assistance in hospitals and other health settings, environmental cleanups, and renovation and construction of homes and community facilities. Tasks also include advocacy and policy-level work on such issues as housing, economic development, the environment, education, and human services. Service-learning programs have different goals and different approaches. For example, curricular programs can view service-learning as discipline-based or as part of general education. Cocurricular programs can have goals of leadership, citizenship, or spiritual development. Reflection components are thus designed to focus on different learning outcomes and to use a wide range of methodologies. As a program type, service-learning encompasses evaluation of its effects on students, as well as on individuals and communities served.

"Reflection components are thus designed to focus on different learning outcomes."

Service-learning is also a philosophy of "human growth and purpose, a social vision, an approach to community, and a way of knowing." It is the element of reciprocity that elevates it to the level of philosophy, "an expression of values—service to others, community development and empowerment, reciprocal learning—which determines the purpose, nature and process of *social and educational exchange* between learners (students) and the people they serve." Service-learning is therefore a philosophy of reciprocity, which implies a concerted effort to move from charity to justice, from service to the elimination of need.

As a pedagogy, service-learning is education that is grounded in experience as a basis for learning and on the centrality and intentionality of reflection designed to enable learning to occur. Based on the work of Dewey, Piaget, and Kurt Lewin, Kolb's concept of the experiential learning cycle is useful in elucidating the role of service-learning as pedagogy. His model outlines the learning experience as a constantly revisited four-step cycle: concrete experience, reflection on the experience, synthesis and abstract conceptualization, and active experimentation—that is, testing the concepts in new situations. Although one may enter the cycle at any point, a person engaged in service-learning often begins with concrete service experience and then embarks on a period of reflection on that experience, analyzing what actually occurred and what implications arise from those observations. In the next step, reflection stimulates the learner to integrate observations and implications with existing knowledge and to formulate concepts and questions to deepen the learner's understanding of the world and the root causes of the need for service. In the fourth step of the model, the learner tests these concepts in different situations. This experimentation leads the learner to begin the cycle again and again. Chapter Three elaborates on Kolb's model and its relevance to service-learning.

Recent discussions in which I have been involved have focused on service-learning as a political stance. With its commitment to social justice, service-learning is clearly not value free. Nevertheless, I believe firmly that proponents and practitioners of service-learning must strenuously avoid directly or indirectly influencing participants toward specific political parties or toward their personally held political views. This type of influence is inappropriate and exclusionary and can adversely affect an institution's willingness to integrate service-learning into its mission and practices.

Higher Education's Tradition of Service

It is important to ground today's concept and practice of service-learning in higher education's long tradition of service. In his preeminent history of higher education, Frederick Rudolph reminds us: "From the beginning, the American college was cloaked with a public purpose, with a responsibility to the past and the present and the future." Since the founding of Harvard College in 1636, the goals of American higher education have included the preparation of citizens for active involvement in community life.

Following the Revolutionary War, the purposes of higher education slowly began to shift from the focus on individual students to the building of a new nation. Rudolph notes that the founding of institutions such as Rensselaer Polytechnic Institute in 1824 responded to the need for builders of railroads, bridges, and other physical and social structures.

In 1862 the passage of the Land-Grant Act inextricably linked higher education and the concept of service, specifically related to agriculture and industry. This linkage led Woodrow Wilson, who would become president of Princeton University in 1902, to state: "It is not learning but the spirit of service that will give a college a place in the annals of the nation." In 1903 David Starr Jordan, president of Stanford University, declared that "the entire university movement, in this country was progressing towards 'reality' and 'practicality.'"

In "Creating the New American College," Boyer contends that this vision of service has been reaffirmed over and over again.

When the economy collapsed, causing the Great Depression, President Franklin D. Roosevelt recruited outstanding scholars to serve as his consultants. During World War II research universities joined with the government to create solutions to new problems. Two important government–higher education partnerships were founded in the war's wake: the National Science Foundation and the GI Bill. Once the Soviet Union launched *Sputnik* in 1957, higher education joined yet another partnership with government, seeking to improve education in primary and secondary schools. And as Boyer points out, "the very title of the National Defense Education Act of 1958 clearly linked higher education to the security of our country."

The Emergence of Service-Learning

"Service-learning established itself and flourished on many college campuses in the late 1960s and the 1970s."

College student community service has a long history that includes the YMCA, 4-H, the Scouting movement, Greek-letter organizations, and many campus ministry initiatives. It grew dramatically in both numbers and in public attention in the 1960s, inspired by President John F. Kennedy's launching of the Peace Corps in 1961. Volunteers in Service to America (VISTA) followed in 1965, engaging young people, mostly college students or recent graduates, to tackle problems within the United States. The civil rights movement of the 1960s challenged both institutions of higher education and students to participate in the burgeoning demand for social justice.

As a form of experiential education, service-learning has its roots in Dewey's theory of experience, which "has become the philosophical touchstone of the experiential movement." Along with internships, cooperative education, and other forms of experiential learning, service-learning established itself and flourished on many college campuses in the late 1960s and the 1970s.

The term *service-learning* first emerged in the work of Sigmon and William Ramsey at the Southern Regional Education Board in 1967. In 1969 the Office of Economic Opportunity established the National Student Volunteer Program, which shortly became the National Center for Service-Learning. Two years later, this program, along with VISTA and the Peace Corps, combined to form the federal agency ACTION. As a national center for student service, ACTION published a magazine, *Synergist*; developed a network; and distributed seed money. One of its projects, the University Year for ACTION, involved more than ten thousand students from over one hundred colleges and universities in the 1970s. Many campus-based service programs were started during this period. Some have vanished, but others still exist. In addition, regional and consortium programs emerged in the 1960s and 1970s, such as the Southern Regional Education Board's resource development internships, the Philadelphia Urban Semester (Great Lakes Colleges of the Midwest), Chicago Urban Semester (Associated Colleges of the Midwest), and the Twin Cities Metropolitan Urban Studies Term and City Arts (Higher

Education Consortium for Urban Affairs, HECUA).

Although the National Center for Service-Learning was relatively short-lived, colleges and universities interested in service-learning continued to network through organizations that developed outside the federal agency. In 1978 the National Society for Internships and Experiential Education (NSIEE; as of 1994, the National Society for Experiential Education, NSEE) was formed by fusing separate groups for field experience education and service internships. NSIEE became the repository and distributor for the considerable written resources on service-learning of the National Center for Service-Learning. Along a parallel track, the Council for Adult and Experiential Learning did much work to lay the foundation for the acceptance of experiential education in colleges and universities.

Lessons Learned from the 1960s and 1970s

The service-learning movement that had acquired a foothold on college campuses in the 1960s and 1970s did not last. Kendall identifies three pitfalls that brought about the demise of many programs that involved college students in service:

1. Most of the programs were not integrated into the central mission and goals of the schools and agencies where they were based....

2. Those in the community service movement learned several important programmatic lessons about the balance of power and the pitfalls of "helping others" or "doing good."...Paternalism, unequal relationships between the parties involved, and a tendency to focus only on charity—"doing for" or "helping" others—rather than on supporting others to meet their own needs all become gaping pitfalls for program after well-intentioned program....

3. We learned that while it sounds great to help young people learn through service experiences in the community, the service experience does not ensure that either significant learning or effective service will occur....

Kendall reports that a number of educators, community leaders, and students who believed in the potential of service learning continued through the "me generation" of the late 1970s and the 1980s to identify the elements that need to be incorporated into successful, sustainable programs. Their work has served to encourage the recent great surge of interest in service-learning by institutions of higher education, students, communities, and the federal government.

Service-Learning Today

In 1985 college student community service gained new momentum. The Education Commission of the States began Campus

Compact: The Project for Public and Community Service. Campus Compact, an organization of college and university presidents who have pledged to encourage and support academically based community service at their institutions, now has over five hundred members. While the presidents were establishing Campus Compact, a group of recent college graduates formed the Campus Outreach Opportunity League (COOL) to encourage students to serve their communities. As a result, many student-initiated service projects were born, and COOL has an ever-expanding national network. COOL works with approximately one thousand colleges and universities, and more than two thousand students attend COOL's annual conferences. COOL's Critical Elements of Thoughtful Community Service have served as guides for the development of hundreds of high-quality community service projects.

"NSEE began a process of articulating and refining a set of principles of good practice in 1987."

From 1983 to 1989 consultants trained by NSEE, with support from the Fund for the Improvement of Postsecondary Education, worked with more than five hundred colleges and universities to develop and strengthen experiential education. The consultations were based on the premises that service-learning (and all other experiential education) must be firmly rooted in the mission of the institution, involve faculty, be integrated into the curriculum, and be grounded in sound theory and pedagogical practice.

In response to the burgeoning growth of community service and service-learning programs and the increasing awareness that effective service and learning do not necessarily happen automatically, NSEE began a process of articulating and refining a set of principles of good practice in 1987. The intense and thorough process culminated in a 1989 Wingspread conference hosted by the Johnson Foundation at which the *Principles of Good Practice in Combining Service and Learning* were hammered out. Although there are numerous definitions of service-learning in wide use today recorded in articles, books, laws, and scholarly and institutional documents, all recent definitions are based on the key statement in the preamble to the Wingspread principles: "Service, combined with learning, adds value to each and transforms both."

On the heels of the Wingspread principles, Kendall and associates published the seminal three-volume set, *Combining Service and Learning*, in 1990, under the auspices of NSEE, in collaboration with ninety-one national and regional associations. It brought together a wide range of resources on service-learning in K-12 settings, as well as higher education, including many previously published and new historical, theoretical, policy-related, practical, and programmatic pieces, plus an annotated bibliography of the service-learning literature. In the same year, Jossey-Bass became the first mainstream educational publisher to produce a volume on service-learning, *Community Service as Values Education*, edited by Cecilia I. Delve, Suzanné D. Mintz, and

Greig M. Stewart.

The 1990s have seen a veritable explosion of literature and conferences on service-learning. In 1991 NSEE sponsored another Wingspread conference, which spawned the *Research Agenda for Combining Service and Learning in the 1990s*. With the support of the Kellogg Foundation, the Office of Community Service Learning at the University of Michigan brought out *Praxis I: A Faculty Casebook on Community Service*; *Praxis II: Service Learning Resources for University Students, Staff and Faculty*; and *Praxis III: Voices in Dialogue*. These volumes focus on curricular service-learning and are valuable for faculty in designing service-learning courses. In response to the call for published research on the effects of service-learning, the *Michigan Journal of Community Service Learning* was launched in fall 1994. In the same year, NSEE published the *Service-Learning Reader: Reflections and Perspectives on Service*, a textbook designed to facilitate students' thoughtful reflection on their service experiences. Campus Compact continues to produce important resources, such as *Rethinking Tradition: Integrating Service with Academic Study*, *Redesigning Curricula: Models of Service Learning Syllabi*, *Service Matters: A Sourcebook for Community Service in Higher Education*, and *Service Counts: Lessons from the Field of Service and Higher Education*.

The national conferences and regular publications of many higher education associations whose primary focus is not service-learning or experiential education have featured large numbers of speakers and articles on service-learning. Among these organizations are the American Association of Higher Education, the Council of Independent Colleges, the United Negro College Fund, the American Association of Community Colleges, the National Association of Student Personnel Administrators, the American College Personnel Association, the National Association of Student Employment Administrators, the National Association of Campus Activities, and the Association of College Unions–International.

The federal government's interest in and support of service-learning increased substantially in the 1990s with the passage of the National and Community Service Trust Act of 1990. This act represented the culmination of George Bush's 1988 presidential campaign recognition of "a thousand points of light," which inspired the creation of the first White House Office of National Service and the Points of Light Foundation. After the excitement created by Bill Clinton's presidential campaign for a large-scale national service program, a long and heated congressional debate finally culminated in the passage of the National and Community Service Trust Act of 1993. As a result, the Commission on National and Community Service, ACTION, and the newly established National Civilian Community Corps merged to form the Corporation for National and Community Service, generally referred to as the Corporation for National Service.

In its first year, the corporation funded the creation of twenty thousand positions in the AmeriCorps national service program, as well as service-learning programs in both K–12 and higher education settings through Learn and Serve America. The corporation's programs have given tremendous impetus to service-learning in colleges and universities. Many institutions of higher education have entered into partnerships with community agencies and schools to engage college students in addressing a wide range of needs. AmeriCorps participants receive living subsidies plus a substantial postservice educational stipend to be used to pay off acquired educational debts or to finance future education and training. In addition, the Higher Education Amendments of 1992 regarding student financial aid stipulated that beginning in July 1994, 5 percent of the federal work-study program funds allocated to each institution must be used to compensate students engaged in community service.

"AmeriCorps participants receive living subsidies plus a substantial postservice educational stipend."

On September 8, 1994, President Clinton wrote a letter to all college and university presidents—the first time any president has ever done so for any reason—asking for their help in "inspiring an ethic of service across our nation." In response to the president's call to service, the American Association of Higher Education and Campus Compact convened the Colloquium on National and Community Service in January 1995. The colloquium has already spawned many additional meetings, workshops, and materials that deal with service-learning in higher education.

Institutional Traditions, Approaches, and Models

Different types of institutions have distinctly different missions, traditions, and approaches regarding service and service-learning. Some embrace service-learning as a philosophy and have developed programs that encompass the critical elements of reflection and reciprocity. Others support student involvement in community service to varying extents and may or may not include the fundamental concepts of service-learning.

At church-related colleges and universities like Notre Dame, Azusa Pacific, Messiah College, and Loyola College in Maryland, service-learning is firmly grounded in the institution's spiritual mission and in the quest for social justice. Other institutions, such as Rutgers, Baylor, and Providence College, have chosen to found their programs primarily on the relationship of service to citizenship, civic responsibility, and participatory democracy. At both private institutions like Stanford, Brown, and Bentley and public ones like Portland State, University of Washington, and Brevard Community College, a center for service-learning links service to academic study. The University of Richmond uses the connection of service and leadership as the basis of its program. The University of Minnesota, the University of Pennsylvania, Miami-Dade Community College, and Gettysburg College, as well as many historically black institutions (Clark Atlanta University, Chicago State University, and Southern University and A&M

College), ground their service-learning programs in community partnerships and public problem solving. Some institutions whose service-learning programs are based on community collaboration are members of consortiums with other colleges and universities, including the Shriver Center Consortium in Baltimore, the Urban Community Service Program in California, and the Regional Action Team in Colorado.

More and more institutions, among them Franklin and Marshall, Portland State, Alverno College, Waynesburg College, and Chandler-Gilbert Community College, have integrated service-learning into the core undergraduate curriculum. Many others envision service-learning as a way to achieve greater depth in a particular field of knowledge. Programs based in student affairs generally emphasize psychosocial, moral, leadership, and citizenship development, together with honing practical skills and deepening students' appreciation of individual differences and commonalties.

Service-learning programs exist at a wide range of levels of institutional commitment. At institutions where service-learning is central, it is a prominent and highlighted aspect of the mission; institutional funding is secure; policies explicitly support service; student, faculty, and staff involvement in service-learning is recognized and rewarded; and a strong commitment to service-learning is shared among all constituents. At the other end of the continuum are many colleges and universities where those who promote and attempt to coordinate service-learning remain on the periphery of their institutions' policies and practices, where funding is scarce and constantly in question, and where those who engage in service-learning feel isolated from the institutional mainstream.

Community service and service-learning programs are housed in various locations on campus. Student organizations were among the first coordinators of service programs, and many continue to be the institution's focal point for service. According to Campus Compact's 1994 survey of its members, offices such as student affairs and student activities are the most common home (45 percent) for service programs. Religious institutions often house their service programs within the campus ministry, and many programs originated with campus ministers in public institutions as well. While some programs are based in career centers and internship offices, an increasing number each year are under the purview of an academic department or dean. And at some colleges and universities, service-learning reports jointly to academic and student affairs, while at others, it reports directly to the president's office.

Programs primarily associated with academic affairs tend to reflect a high institutional commitment; result in a more centralized, coordinated program; and risk overemphasizing learning and under-emphasizing service. Programs housed in student affairs tend to be more flexible in responding to student needs and more open to student initiatives; respond more effectively to community needs; risk overemphasizing service and underemphasizing learning; are often of a lower priority to the institution and less stable financially; and are linked with only one academic department, if any. Regardless of where service-learning is administratively located, it is the premise of this book that If service-learning is to be central rather than marginal, it must be integrated into both academic and cocurricular practice.

Moving from Community
Service to Service-Learning

Observers of higher education and contemporary society strongly believe that higher education has a rich array of resources and tremendous potential to make a significant positive difference in meeting growing human needs and in addressing increasingly complex social and economic problems. However, although the public, together with many federal and state officials, may believe that colleges and universities are blessed with underworked faculty, fat operating budgets, and abundant staff, the reality is to the contrary. In what is actually a time of reduced public support, soaring costs, decaying infrastructures, and everdiversifying student bodies with greater needs for services, institutions of higher education are thinking strategically about what they can and cannot do. More and more are harkening back to their fundamental missions and focusing more sharply on their primary purposes.

This is why this…is about service-learning rather than student volunteer or community service. If higher education is to sustain its historical commitment to service in this time of great societal needs and increased competition among its own priorities, it is essential that developing opportunities for students to engage in service-learning must also enable colleges and universities to meet their own educational goals for students. Although community service has generally been perceived as a good thing, all good things cannot be the province of higher education. Service-learning, with its intentional goals for student learning and development, fits far more clearly into higher education's mission and priorities than volunteer or community service programs, which lack its reflection component and intentional learning goals.

The higher education community has turned much attention to the need to strengthen the quality of undergraduate education. There are concerns about fragmented and incoherent curricula, lack of clarity about purposes and goals, absence of values, the need to integrate out-of-class experiences with education, and the need to prepare students better for the world of work. The Wingspread Group on Higher Education identifies at least three fundamental issues common to all U.S. colleges and universities: "taking values seriously; putting student learning first; and creating a nation of learners." As a means of addressing these issues, the group recommends that colleges and universities organize and sustain community service programs for large numbers of students and "wholeheartedly commit themselves to providing students with opportunities to experience and reflect on the world beyond the campus." Boyer proposes judging the quality of a college education by asking if "students see the connection between what they learn and how they live, looking for the deeper significance, for the moral dilemmas and the ethical responses." He goes on to say that "the college succeeds as its graduates are inspired by a larger vision, using the knowledge they have acquired to form values and advance the common good." Chickering and Gamson articulate seven principles for the improvement of undergraduate education, which point clearly toward service-learning:

Good practice in undergraduate education:
1. Encourages student-faculty contact.
2. Encourages cooperation among students.
3. Encourages active learning.
4. Gives prompt feedback.
5. Emphasizes time on task.
6. Communicates high expectations.
7. Respects diverse talents and ways of learning.

Another goal that service-learning effectively addresses is citizenship education and preparation for participation in a democracy. According to Frank Newman, "If there is a crisis in education in the United States today, it is less that test scores have declined than it is that we have failed to provide the education for citizenship that is still the most significant responsibility of the nation's schools and colleges." It is virtually impossible to "teach" students what it means to be a citizen or to participate in democracy. "People cannot be told how to be responsible, knowledgeable, or caring citizens. They must be involved in the process." Astin cites service-learning as the most effective means of accomplishing higher education's "stated mission: to produce educated citizens who understand and appreciate not only how democracy is supposed to work but also their own responsibility to become active and informed participants in it."

Besides preparing students for citizenship and democratic participation, higher education's goals include preparing them for the world of work. Academic knowledge cannot be successfully applied without well-developed cognitive and social skills. In addition, students must acquire a set of transferable skills rather than prepare for a single lifelong career. Service-learning affords students opportunities to develop such skills as the ability to synthesize information, creative problem solving, constructive teamwork, effective communication, well-reasoned decision making, and negotiation and compromise. Other qualities that can be developed through service-learning include initiative, flexibility and adaptability openness, and empathy. Service-learning in professional education leads to an increased sense of social responsibility on the part of physicians, lawyers, business leaders, government officials, and other key practitioners and decision makers.

Another shared goal among institutions of higher education is to develop students' appreciation of human differences and commonalties and to teach individuals to live peacefully and productively in communities that value persons of different races, genders, physical and mental abilities, religions, class backgrounds, and sexual orientations. Service-learning, which has as basic tenets reciprocity among those who are servers and those who are served and a reflective component with intentional learning goals, helps participants develop a deeper understanding of these issues, as well as how values and norms are socially constructed and the causes of social injustice.

It is unwise and inexpedient to propose a blueprint or model for institutional programs that involve college students in service to the local, national, and global communities. However, it is clearly in the best interest of students, communities, and institutions alike if higher education commits itself to service-learning rather than to community service and volunteer programs lacking service-learning's principles, which so clearly enable colleges and universities to meet their already established educational goals.

Conclusion

This chapter began by defining service-learning and clarifying its distinctions from volunteerism and community service. It has discussed higher education's tradition of service, the emergence of service-learning, and an overview of service-learning at today's colleges and universities. This introduction has also affirmed that service-learning is both curricular and cocurricular and can be designed to yield a wide range of outcomes for student learning and development, as well as for community enhancement. Service learning is in fact a significant means through which higher education can achieve its overarching goals. Service-learning activities, be they course based or not, one-time or intensive, merit such designation if they include the basic elements of structured reflection and reciprocity.

The Millennium Project: Fifty Ways to Make a Difference[4]

Simple acts of generosity and kindness are the greatest gifts of all. Here's how to lend a helping hand—and feel good about yourself.

"Citizen service...is an American idea that every American should embrace," says President Bill Clinton. "[Problems] can be solved only when we come together to lift each other up—a person at a time, a family at a time, a neighborhood at a time, a school at a time."

This April, Clinton and former President George Bush plan to lead the country in an effort to do just that. In Philadelphia, Clinton and Bush, joined by former presidents, will convene The Presidents' Summit for America's Future, a conference intended to bring America to a new level of commitment to volunteerism. The summit will focus on children—helping those in need, and encouraging all kids to become involved in community service. The main goal is to inspire individuals and organizations to make volunteer work "an integral part of the American way of life."

The summit will be chaired by General Colin Powell and spearheaded by the Points of Light Foundation, a nonprofit organization dedicated to volunteer community service, and the Corporation for National Service, a federal agency that provides opportunities for people to serve their communities. Local and national leaders will announce specific community-service goals for the organizations they represent. Then, delegations from all fifty states will go to work on turning those commitments into action. "Stretching volunteer service from one ocean to the other in this country can help turn the tide in improving the lives of our young people," Powell told the *Journal*. "I urge others to join in this worthy effort."

April 1997 is also a "cosmic" month. April 6 begins the countdown of 1,000 days before the year 2000. So, inspired by The Presidents' Summit and by the approach of a new century, *Ladies' Home Journal* has launched an ongoing community-service campaign called The Millenium Project, in association with the Points of Light Foundation. Mirroring the goals of the summit, we want to encourage you to give 1,000 of something before the year 2000; it can be anything from 1,000 pennies collected by your children and donated to their favorite charity to 1,000 minutes of your time spent working at a homeless shelter (see "How to Give 1,000 Things," p.32). Then, write and tell us about your volunteer activities. In future issues, we will feature the inspiring

"The main goal is to inspire individuals and organizations to make volunteer work 'an integral part of the American way of life.'"

---

4 Article by Lynn Harris from *Ladies' Home Journal* 114:140-3 My '97. Copyright © 1997 Meredith Corporation. All rights reserved. Reprinted with the permission of *Ladies' Home Journal.*

individuals and families who have dedicated themselves to volunteerism—and suggest more ways in which a few moments of your time can make a millennium of difference.

The Greatest Givers

Meet some very special people whose dedication and hard work has changed the lives of others.

Teaching by Example

Imagine a school where the staff has to *ask* students to leave the building by six P.M. A school in a bleak urban area with a community vegetable garden and a mini-farm. A school with only thirty-five students (pre–K through 12), a waiting list of nearly seven hundred and a sliding-scale tuition system. Where parents donate at least ten volunteer hours every month, and the seniors all go on to some form of higher learning, most of them to college. A school whose principal and head teacher works all day, every day, for no pay at all.

That school is the Sheenway School and Culture Center, in South Central Los Angeles, and that principal and head teacher is Dolores Sheen. "We try to make Sheenway like the old-fashioned one-room schoolhouse at the center of town, where everyone helps out and everyone is extended family," says Sheen, fifty-nine, who founded the school with her late father in 1971.

The students take an active role in their education. They attend board meetings and meet with and evaluate prospective students. (There are no set academic requirements for entrance; students are admitted on a first-come, first-serve basis.) They also give something back: Younger pupils volunteer their time on campus and off, and high schoolers are required to do a community-service project every semester.

For her part, Sheen, who has been known to work a seven-day, ninety-hour week, also pitches in as cook, janitor, nurse and counselor at a school that has never received government funding. But help comes in other ways. Her five grown children and some friends pay her living expenses, two part-time teachers work for free and community members—as well as celebrities such as Jodie Foster, Richard Pryor and Lionel Richie—donate their time, money or both to Sheenway's classrooms and coffers. (Sheen, a 1996 recipient of the President's Service Award, currently dreams of a $20 million renovation and expansion so she can accommodate up to 250 students.)

"Money is always good, but we never forget the people who come to the school, talk to the students and pitch in," Sheen says. "That way the children get to see people and things they can aspire to be and do. That's the kind of attention and inspiration they need every day."

Family Ties

What started as a way for one family to spend more time together has brought two families together.

"My husband, Ken, and I had always volunteered, but that meant time away from our kids," says Maureen Moo-Dodge, forty-four, an at-home mom in Minneapolis with two daughters, Jessica, fourteen, and Lauren, eleven.

Their solution: volunteer together—with the goal of making new friends. That's what led Maureen to Family-to-Family Ties, a Minneapolis organization that pairs families to create friendships and support networks.

The Moo-Dodges were matched with Gale Allen and her sons, Tony, eleven; Christopher, seven; and Ke'Shawn, three. At least once a month, the families bake pies or go to the park and try in-line skating. Occasionally, Ken spends "guy" time with Tony, who seems most to crave a male role model in his life. Sometimes, Gale and Maureen just talk.

"They give me the inspiration I need to handle being a single parent—and to know that I am a good mother," says Gale, thirty-three, who works in a women's shelter. "They do it from the heart."

The Moo-Dodges say they get back more than they give. "Gale sets a great example for us," says Maureen. "Her mothering techniques are extraordinary."

The families' partnership has also widened the children's eyes to differences—both significant and superficial—and taught them how much they have in common. Says Jessica, "We're two families that like to have fun and do the same things. Our backgrounds are different, but that doesn't matter when we're together."

Most of all, says Maureen, "Ken and I have realized how easy—and lonely—it is to get lost in the shuffle. We can get so busy that we don't stop and see what's happening around us." But the Moo-Dodges have found a way. Recently, they started a photo album for Gale and the boys. "Gale just cried when she saw it," Maureen says. "They didn't have recent photographs of their family—something we take for granted. I see our life differently now."

A Teen with a Mission

Emily New is as comfortable walking into the Capitol to lobby for a bill as she is walking along the highway to pick up litter. At nineteen, she already has a longstanding dedication to all sorts of volunteerism, from working directly with those in need to setting policy at a national level. For her, community service is central to her life.

"My idea of service has evolved," says Emily, now a first-year student at Trinity University, in San Antonio. "When I was younger I thought, What can I do for others? I've come to see how important it is to help people accomplish things for themselves."

Emily started volunteering when she was twelve. She became an ambassador for the Children's Alliance for the Protection of the Environment, speaking before school audiences, politicians and even a U.N. Youth Forum. But she was eventually drawn to working directly with people. She joined her school's support group for children of alcoholics (her mother is recovering) and gave presentations to teachers and principals about how a student's performance might be affected by a home life colored by alcoholism.

Emily then trained to become a mentor to middle-school students at risk of failing, or worse. She talked to them about everything from improving study skills to handling suicidal thoughts. She has also gone into high-school classrooms to educate students about AIDS.

Emily, a 1996 recipient of the Yoshiyama award for Exemplary Service to the Community, sponsored by the Hitachi Foundation, now belongs to Alpha Phi Omega (APO), a national co-ed fraternity whose mission is community service. With APO, she tutors high-school students, cleans an "adopted" stretch of highway and serves as a den parent to a troop of deaf Cub Scouts.

She is also making a difference at the national level. She was recently elected to the National Council on Youth Policy, which tracks and lobbies for legislation affecting America's young people. "It's important for us to be involved in our communities and in decisions that affect us," says Emily. "Although we're not all old enough to vote, young people are members of society like everyone else. We're not 'training' to start living—we are living."

How to Give 1,000 Things

So, have we inspired you to become a volunteer? Join The Millennium Project and donate 1,000 of something—whether it's minutes, pennies or even smiles—before the year 2000. Here are some ideas to get you started.

On Your Own or with Your Family—Give:

- *1,000 minutes of companionship.* Bring cheer to a nursing home for a few hours every week.

- *1,000 songs.* Lead a monthly sing-along at a hospital.

- *1,000 pages.* Read to children at a homeless shelter or hospital.

- *1,000 milligrams of caffeine.* Give up your afternoon cappuccino for a month and save the money for your favorite charity.

- *1,000 good wishes.* With your kids, make greeting cards for the nursing-home bound.

- *1,000 words.* Offer to help teenagers with college application essays.

- *1,000 math problems.* Or, tutor kids in math or algebra.

- *1,000 days as a role model.* Join a Big Brothers/Big Sisters program.

- *1,000 pennies.* Encourage your children to save for a charity they care about.

- *1,000 square inches of storage space.* Clean out the garage, and give away outgrown bikes and sports equipment.

- *1,000 signatures.* Circulate a petition concerning an issue that is important to you.

- *1,000 hugs.* Spend time at the hospital holding the failure-to-thrive babies whose survival may depend on simple human contact.

- *1,000 calls for help.* Train to staff a crisis hotline.

- *1,000 files.* Remodeling your office? Offer discarded cabinets and shelves to a nonprofit organization.

- *1,000 nickels.* Encourage children to collect cans and bottles, and donate the deposits to charity.

- *1,000 ways to worship.* Arrange an "exchange" program with a family of a different religion: Have them over for your next holiday celebration, then join them for theirs.

- *1,000 foreign words.* If you speak a foreign language, offer to tutor students.

- *1,000 winners.* Volunteer to work at your local Special Olympics program.

- *1,000 minutes of parental involvement.* Offer to spend time helping out at your child's school.

- *1,000 ripples.* Share ideas for community service with others.

With Your Friends, Give:

- *1,000 brushstrokes.* Gather to repaint a classroom.

- *1,000 miles.* Offer to run errands for the home-bound—or drive them where they need to go.

- *1,000 odd jobs.* Suggest that the neighborhood kids organize an after-school odd-jobs pool—it's a great way to keep the community beautiful.

- *1,000 ccs of blood.* Donate a unit of blood at the local blood drive—and bring a friend along to do the same (500 ccs of blood equals about one unit).

- *1,000 hostess gifts.* Whenever you and your friends entertain, ask guests to bring one item for the local food pantry

- *1,000 days of safety.* Volunteer to lend a hand at a shelter for battered women.

- *1,000 brighter moments.* Regularly visit a hospice.

Team with Your Company to Give:

- *1,000 (paid) hours.* Ask your company to encourage employees to devote a paid work day to performing community service.

- *1,000 megs of RAM.* Donate old office computers to a local nonprofit organization.

- *$1,000.* Make a deal with your CEO—if the employees in your office can raise $500 for charity, the company will match it.

- *1,000 meals.* Commit with your co-workers to help serve meals at a soup kitchen.

- *1,000 calories.* Ask your co-workers to give up their afternoon candy bars and turn the savings over to a charity.

- *1,000 pieces of litter.* Get your office to adopt a park and help keep it clean.

- *1,000 smiles.* Take a group of underprivileged children to the circus.

- *1,000 nails.* Organize a carpentry-repair team for a leaky school roof.

- *1,000 tea leaves.* With co-workers, host a tea party at a local nursing home.

- *1,000 seeds.* Organize your colleagues to landscape a vacant lot.

- *1,000 loving homes.* Offer to help find new families for the animals at the pound.

Work with a Community Organization to Collect:

- *1,000 items of clothing.* Place bins at stores to collect clothes for the needy.

- *1,000 coats.* Start a coat drive now for those who may be cold next winter.

- *1,000 shoes.* Do the same with shoes that are still in good shape.

- *1,000 cans.* Ask grocery shoppers to buy extra canned goods for the local food pantry. Collect donations as they leave the store.

- *1,000 toys.* Collect toys for the hospital's pediatric ward.

- *1,000 blankets.* Start a blanket drive for a homeless shelter.

- *1,000 baskets.* Organize a kids' basketball shoot-a-thon, with sponsors donating $1 per basket to local youth sports.

- *1,000 or so jellybeans.* Hold a count-the-jellybeans-in-the-jar raffle for charity.

- *1,000 laughs.* Organize a comedy night to raise money for charity.

- *1,000 sweets.* Sponsor a bake sale for a local volunteer organization.

> - *1,000 suds.* Hold a neighborhood car wash for a local shelter.
> - *1,000 kilometers.* Organize 100 people to run a 10K race for charity.

Volunteering: It's on the Upswing

About 93 million adults ages eighteen and up volunteered in 1995—an increase of 4 million since 1993. Thirty-five- to fifty-four-year-olds were the most likely to give their time, followed by those twenty-five to thirty-four.

In 1995, volunteers gave an average of 4.2 hours per week.

Americans devoted an estimated total of 20.3 billion hours to both formal and informal volunteering (such as helping out a neighbor) in 1995.

Eighty-five percent of those now doing volunteer work are working on one or more serious social problems. Of that group, 55 percent help the elderly; 46 percent volunteer for a child- or youth-related problem.

More women than men volunteer (52 percent versus 45 percent). Women are more likely to serve on boards and committees; provide companionship to the lonely; tutor children; provide child care or substitute parenting; make, deliver or serve meals; and do office work for volunteer organizations.

Men are more likely to offer counseling and advice to those in need, participate in recreation-oriented activities, get involved with neighborhood cleanup efforts and provide planning, administration and leadership to organizations.

How to Get Started

You want to volunteer, but aren't sure where to begin? Here, a few helpful tips.

Is there a particular expertise that you have to offer? Computer experts, for example, might be able to help train teachers and students in the use of new classroom technology.

Would you like to do something that's different from the way you normally spend your time? If you work alone in a home office, you might want to find a project that puts you in the midst of lots of people. Or, if you direct a lot of traffic during the day, perhaps you would prefer to do some quieter behind-the-scenes work.

What are you really passionate about? Find something you care deeply about. Don't select a project just because you feel you "should" or because it's the "right thing."

What kind of time commitment can you realistically make? One way that busy people fit in volunteer work is by working a set schedule—such as tutoring every Monday from six to seven P.M.

To find out what opportunities are available in your community, call your local hospital's community affairs office, church or synagogue with community-outreach program, the school system—or just look around your neighborhood see how you could make a difference.

Call the Points of Light Foundation's Volunteer Information Line at 800-595-4448 to find a Points of Light Volunteer Center near you. They'll match you up with an organization that needs your help.

Volunteers Fail to Heed
Clinton's Call[5]

Summit Produces Few Results

Back in April, at the volunteerism summit in Philadelphia, President Clinton stood with three former presidents and retired General Colin Powell and declared in no vague terms, "We are here because I want to redefine the meaning of citizenship in America."

While rock stars sang for the crowds and old political enemies blurred battle lines in the name of a higher cause, it appeared that Vice President Al Gore might be right when he described the gathering as the launch of a "dramatic national effort."

But nearly six months later, many leaders and front-line workers in the nation's nonprofit industry say that the highly touted summit has barely caused a blip in the number of people volunteering, never mind a redefinition of any sort.

They complain that summit leaders have done little to pursue their ambitious goals. They also say that Clinton has spoken on volunteerism precious few times, and in relatively low-profile settings, since leaving the klieg lights of Philadelphia behind.

"I don't think it was a failure, but I don't think it was a seminal event," said Jeremy Rifkin, president of the Foundation of Economic Trends in Washington. "The president could be using this as a bully pulpit. Reagan certainly did. Bush did. Clinton has done nothing since."

Said Julian Wolpert, a Princeton University professor and expert on philanthropy: "I don't see much follow-through."

On the streets, from the homeless shelters of Massachusetts to the mentoring programs in San Francisco, executives and activists in the nonprofit industry say they saw none of the expected surge in volunteers after the Philadelphia event. To them, the glitz of the summit failed to translate to the grinding work of volunteerism.

"It didn't have a huge impact," said Paul Denning, a spokesman at the Pine Street Inn, a Boston homeless shelter. Added John Scherer, the program director for the Big Brother/Big Sisters of Marin County, Calif., of his post-summit recruitment: "It wasn't significantly different than what we would have in any given month."

Likewise with many large national organizations. At the United Way of America, spokesman Don Struke simply said, "I have heard nothing myself." At the highly successful Youth Service

---

5 Article by Brian McGrory, staffwriter, from the *Boston Globe* O 12 '97. Copyright
© 1997 *Boston Globe*. Reprinted courtesy of the *Boston Globe*.

America, Steven Culbertson, one of the most enthusiastic supporters of the summit, has realized few results.

"I'm not seeing a huge jump, or hearing about people banging down doors," Culbertson said. "We run a volunteer Web site, the largest site on the Internet on volunteering. But we haven't seen our hits go through the roof since the summit."

Ann Kaplan, the research director for the American Association of Fund-Raising Counsel, said the non-profit groups represented by her organization watched the summit come and go with little impact in volunteers or financial contributions. She and others said that many of the highly touted corporate commitments announced at the summit had actually been promised months before.

"Clinton founded the highly successful Corporation for National Service in his first term, which includes the AmeriCorps program."

"We have not seen a marked increase that we have noticed," Kaplan said. "The thing that makes people volunteer is being part of a community of commitment, where you care about the organization. It is not a top-down type of thing."

For Clinton, the failed expectations on volunteerism parallel another round of criticism he has received on his race relations initiative. In June, he launched what he called a year-long "national conversation" on race issues. But four months into the program, his advisory board has done little more than hire a staff. Its one meeting with the president appeared so unfocused that Clinton left 15 minutes before his allotted time had expired, apparently for lack of anything else to say.

At the White House, aides staunchly defend Clinton's performance on volunteerism, and history supports their contention that he arrives at the issue with some authority. Clinton founded the highly successful Corporation for National Service in his first term, which includes the Americorps program.

Since the summit, the administration has completed many of Clinton's smaller volunteerism goals. They include: implementing a mentoring program at the Pentagon, a food recovery summit at the Department of Agriculture, an alliance between the Department of Health and Human Services and the Girl Scouts of America, an expanded scholarship program for Americorps volunteers, and a program that waives student loan interest payments for a year if recipients perform volunteer work.

Clinton has devoted one brief speech to volunteerism since April—a radio address in late July. And he occasionally has woven the concept of community service into other speeches, most notably in an address to the U.S. Conference of Mayors in San Francisco in late June.

"It is a theme he believes in," said Ann Lewis, the White House Communications director. "We build it into a lot of what we are doing to heighten interest."

Still, aides are acutely aware of the criticisms, which began even before the summit, when many sociologists declared the event a public relations stunt rather than a substantive policy initiative.

"He's been busy on a number of fronts," said Harris Wofford, the chief executive officer of the Corporation for National Service, explaining the lack of attention. "I feel confident in the next three years that he will use the bully pulpit of the White House very effectively. The White House is actively working with us to plan how to do it and where and when to do it."

Around the country, many of the communities and states that sent delegations to Philadelphia are just now planning local summits, where activists said much of the real work of spurring volunteerism will take place. Massachusetts will have a summit in Boston on Oct. 26.

"There was some cynicism going into Philadelphia that it would be a cameo performance for the cameras, and a number of us were skeptical that this was more PR than substance," said Ira Jackson, executive vice president of BankBoston, one of the summit's main sponsors. "But it is a reinvigorated citizenship we are talking about. The fault, if things don't get done, will lie with those missing in action at the state and local level."

Around the country, many local activists praise Powell, who continues to travel widely and speak at many of the state summits to inspire people toward greater action.

In Washington, the spokesman of America's Promise, the 35-employee organization that Powell formed to follow up on the summit's goals, said the program was proceeding "unbelievably well." But asked for specific numbers of commitments and volunteers, he declined, saying organizers did not plan to unveil those until later this month.

The group has been quietly criticized by some in the movement as disorganized. Indeed, in less than six months, it has already seen the departures of two chairmen—one full-time, the second an interim choice. It is now headed by noted philanthropist Ray Chambers, who guards his privacy.

"America's Promise seems to be a one-man band at this point, with Colin Powell out talking and gathering commitments," said Paul Clolery, editor in chief of the *NonProfit Times*, a trade publication that closely monitors the industry. "Whether they're getting those commitments, I don't know."

Disorganization is a notorious problem among nonprofit groups, where budgets are often razor thin and staffs are frequently over-worked. Many such groups that are the most in need of volunteers are the most inept at putting volunteers to work, organizers said, largely because they do not have strong programs with clear goals and supervision.

Without a good infrastructure behind them, many volunteers become frustrated and quit or cannot find appropriate volunteer work.

"The summit served a great service in getting the message out there," said Kathy Behrens, executive director of New York Cares, a volunteer placement group with chapters in cities around the country, including Boston. "But one thing that needs follow-up,

"Many local activists praise [Colin] Powell, who continues to travel widely and speak at many of the state summits."

and one thing that wasn't addressed, is where those volunteering opportunities are.

"It's not enough to say, 'Volunteer, be a mentor.' It's not enough. You have to make sure they are meaningful opportunities."

Many summit organizers, seeing no immediate surge in volunteering, now say that it will be a long, methodical process in building a culture of greater service. Wofford, for one, said he is frustrated having the summit's success measured in hard numbers. Others agree, shucking off the notion that the greatest chance for success comes in the wake of the massive publicity of the summit.

"One of the byproducts of a spectacular and unique event is the possibility of failed expectations," said Robert Goodwin, the president of the Points of Light Foundation in Washington. "I'm sure that many nonprofits hoped that an occasion such as this would result in more immediate signs of support in volunteer hours and cash donations. I would say that it is unrealistic to expect an avalanche of response."

Push for Volunteerism
Brings No Outpouring[6]

Lorraine Bodden did not show up for work yesterday at KPMG Peat Marwick, the giant accounting firm. Instead, she danced with patients at the Mary Manning Walsh Nursing Home's "autumn ball" in Manhattan, one of 20,000 KPMG employees in 130 offices across the country who got the day off with pay to volunteer at schools, hospitals, nursing homes, parks and youth centers.

KPMG is one of 300 companies and dozens of nonprofit organizations that have begun to fulfill their pledges, made six months ago at the Summit for America's Future in Philadelphia, spearheaded by Gen. Colin L. Powell, President Clinton and three former Presidents, to spend $1 billion and volunteer countless hours to help two million children by 2000.

Yet KPMG's "World of Spirit Day" was planned more than a year before the April meeting, executives said, and the only change in plans arising from that gathering was a stronger emphasis on programs for youth.

KPMG is not alone. Many companies responding to Mr. Clinton's call for a "nation of volunteers" promised to undertake activities they were already doing or at least planning, interviews show.

But while some volunteer and social-service groups around the country report a surge of interest, there is little evidence as yet of masses of individuals coming forward nationwide. "I haven't noticed an outpouring of people who want to volunteer," said David Saltzman, executive director of the Robin Hood Foundation, an innovative New York philanthropy that supports smaller programs for youth and the urban poor.

And some wonder whether volunteerism is the best use of America's philanthropic resources to solve major social problems.

Jon Van Til, professor of urban studies, who directs Rutgers University's Citizenship and Service Education Program in Camden, N.J., questioned whether the $20 million that KPMG sacrificed on Monday's day off would have done more good in the form of a check. "Wouldn't it have been better if Peat Marwick went to these orgnizations and said, 'You've got a choice—a $1,000-a-day accountant doing a $5-an-hour job picking up trash, or a gift of $1,000.'" "Many organizations," he said, would "quickly take the money."

Assessing the impact of volunteerism after the Philadelphia meeting is complicated by the dearth of verifiable data about

"Some wonder whether volunteerism is the best use of America's philanthropic resources."

---

what some 93 million volunteers and companies are really doing or spending, as opposed to what they claim.

"Methods of tracking what's happening in the nonprofit sector are very haphazard," said Alan J. Abramson, director of the Aspen Institute's Nonprofit Sector Research Fund in Washington. "I can tell you the employment rate. But there is no volunteer rate or Dow Jones index for the health of the nonprofit sector."

Part of the problem is that the meeting's organizers, who are supposed to insure that companies meet their pledges, have been in some confusion. America's Promise: The Alliance for Youth, created to encourage and monitor the response to the call for volunteerism on behalf of children, has had two directors and has been hampered by problems ranging from telephones that did not work properly for four months to delays in mailing out questionaires designed to track companies' volunteer efforts. Moreover, the group, operating on a $750,000 budget, has no way of verifying the information companies provide.

Still, with national attention focused on volunteerism, at least a dozen major American companies, including Oracle, Microsoft, NationsBank and Timberland, have made huge new commitments of time, products and money to meet the meeting's goals, sometimes without even informing its organizers. The Philadelphia gathering has also sparked about 150 "mini-summits" at the state and local level, which experts say are likely to be important in boosting volunteerism and meeting goals in the longer term.

"Thanks to the summit, we are no longer an army of 350,000 soldiers each with his own plan for the best way to take the hill," said Raymond G. Chambers, an intensely press-shy philanthropist who helped plan the meeting. "We now have an overarching plan and quantifiable goals."

Mr. Chambers, who is now chief executive officer of America's Promise, also said the evidence was "overwhelming" that volunteerism, and the mentoring of at-risk children, in particular, are among the most effective means of preventing drug abuse, teenage pregnancy, truancy and delinquency.

But Mr. Abramson, of the Aspen Institute, said that managing volunteers is among philanthropy's most difficult tasks. "There is no guarantee that volunteers will show up where they are most needed," he said. "And agencies have to be prepared to handle them."

Initial response to the meeting's call for volunteerism was not overwhelming, said Anne E. Kaplan, research director of Giving USA, which monitors nonprofit giving. A July survey of 580 nonprofit organizations by the *NonProfit Times*, a monthly trade publication, found that only a small number had experienced an increase in the numbers of inquiries about volunteering following the summit meeting. Paul Clolery, the editor, said that while the numbers have picked up in some places, "the challenge is enabling gifts and volunteers to get into the hands of nonprofits.

The delivery systems are simply not in place."

Even the successful marriage of volunteers with organizations can create problems, said Thomas M. McKenna, national executive director of Big Brothers/Big Sisters of America. "Businesses have a much easier time helping us with people than with dollars for infrastructure," he said. "They think all we need are volunteers showing up. But we also need hard dollars to hire the staff to carry out programs."

Mary Prchal, who heads Chicago Cares, of City Cares of America, a network matching volunteers with projects, said there was no shortage of donations in her city, "but the individual is not coming out." She added, "Maybe it's a Midwest thing."

At New York Cares, meanwhile, calls [for an] increase, but staff members said a network television news report call[ed] it a "model" program that may have helped more than the meeting. And in Los Angeles, the agency saw no increase in either volunteers or donations, and none of 250 people who volunteered since April listed the gathering as a reason.

William H. Shore, the head of an anti-hunger group in Washington who helped organize the summit meeting, said America's Promise has tried to distinguish between new corporate commitments and merely repackaged ones. For example, the Walt Disney Company, among others, was initially told that its commitments were not sufficiently new or improved to merit special mention. So Disney expanded its effort by pledging to match 425 Disney stores with Boys and Girls Clubs in 200 cities, he said.

"Corporations don't give anything away to anybody unless they get back in public relations and advertising at least as much as the gift is worth."

Stuart H. Shapiro, a physician and businessman who was the meeting's chief executive, added that the organizers had also rejected multimillion dollar donations for the $4 million gathering from cigarette manufacturers. "The summit's message was children," he said. "You don't want to divert the message."

Mr. Van Til, at Rutgers, said much of what the companies were doing was less philanthropy than "cause-related marketing."

"Corporations don't give anything away to anybody unless they get back in public relations and advertising at least as much as the gift is worth," he said.

But Andrew M. Mecca, director of a statewide mentoring initiative in California to which Oracle Corporation is contributing, says, "If Oracle benefits by benefiting millions of kids across the country, more power to them," he said. "If a company's business grows because it's doing good things for the community, maybe that's healthy."

Responding to the Call

A sampling of corporate responses to the summit meeting in Philadelphia last April calling for a national campaign of volunteerism.

Columbia/HCA—Immunizing one million children by the year 2000.

Microsoft—Providing $200 million in software to public libraries.

Nationsbank—Opening 25 centers for school children and the elderly.

Oracle—Providing $100 million in computers to public schools; electronically linking mentors to students in California.

Pfizer—Donating $2 million more to children's health groups, $1 million in volunteer efforts and $2 million in pediatric medicines.

Scholastic—Providing one million books by the year 2000 to reading programs for children.

VH1—Leading drive to donate one million musical instruments to elementary schools.

II. Private Volunteering and AmeriCorps

Editor's Introduction

Many people in America want to help others. However, wanting to help others and being able to do so are two different things. As times grow more difficult, volunteers as well as governments, local or otherwise, having been withdrawing their support. Yet, while government bodies and tasks are increasing at an enormous rate, these agencies plan to absorb more volunteers, especially those from church and religious nonprofit organizations. Section II is divided into two parts: the first addresses this struggle between government agencies and smaller charity organizations, and the second focuses on AmeriCorps, which is a national service that is meeting resistance among smaller charities and taxpayers.

A volunteer organization called New York Cares offers people the chance to help many of the homeless and underprivileged children of New York City. Tamar Lewin, writing in the *New York Times*, advises newly recruited volunteers of things to be aware of when donating time and effort to charity. With experienced volunteers vital to its success, Big Brothers/Big Sisters, another charity organization for children, has, according to Lewin, had trouble finding many qualified candidates. Often there are problems of matching the need with good intentions, especially when the intention is there, but the infrastructure falls short.

Faced with budget cutbacks, especially in the area of social assistance, understaffed government-funded organizations usually succumb to red tape, and individual cases don't get enough attention. However, in an article from *Reason* magazine, Amy L. Sherman presents a personal story from a volunteer who works where this is not true. The Community-Directed Assistance Program in Maryland receives government funds in a lump sum, and it is the volunteers working together who distribute the funds and help recipients find stable, permanent work. Many charity groups in this country are making it work, linking welfare recipients with small church support groups, creating a partnership between the local government and the religious community.

Meanwhile, as government agencies are enjoying the cooperation of these smaller charities, private organizations are trying to find new ways to have a larger role, even when some voters and policymakers continue to demand cutbacks. In the next article, "The Smart Samaritan," James L. Payne contends that less government funding and more social assistance in the hands of nonprofit organizations like churches and volunteer groups could prove to be a dangerous mix. Some communities, he alleges, do not always keep in mind important principles when devising these charities, and Payne believes that if the private sector were to remain with this approach the country "could end up with a welfare regime just as dysfunctional as the one we are struggling to replace."

AmeriCorps is larger than most nonprofit organizations. By changing its volunteers, teaching the right values, uniting people of different backgrounds, and expanding educational opportunities, it performs useful work, which in the end is the most important thing. The last three articles of Section II are devoted to the impact that AmeriCorps has had on the country. President Bill Clinton appointed Harris Wofford to run AmeriCorps and reorganize the federally funded volunteer and service programs. Wofford and his associates have set out to help not only AmeriCorps but also former president George Bush's Points of Light Foundation with a re-energized spirit of volunteerism. Wofford wants to rebuild the bipartisan support for national service by "link[ing] national service to a national strategy for addressing deep-seated social needs," according to David Gergen for *U.S. News & World Report*; only then, Wofford believes, will we make real progress.

Harris Wofford, CEO of the Corporation for National Service, and Steven Waldman, author of *The Bill*, discuss in their article from *Policy Review* the positive aspects of AmeriCorps. Quoting leaders of 24 volunteer groups as having written that AmeriCorps is an "enormously beneficial addition to the traditional voluntary sector," Wofford and Waldman argue that "volunteers need to be trained, supervised, and deployed well to be effective." By providing that service, AmeriCorps has maximized the productivity of such nonprofit groups as Habitat for Humanity, according to the authors, and in doing so has accomplished the twin goals of helping those in need while benefiting volunteers and AmeriCorps workers alike. Moreover, it enjoys nationwide, biparitsan support despite the complaints of some congressional Republicans, who in this case find themselves, according to Wofford and Waldman, "on the wrong side not only of politics—AmeriCorps is popular with voters—but of their own ideology.... AmeriCorps teaches the right values: ...hard work, discipline, and teamwork that make young people not only more productive workers but also better citizens."

With smaller nonprofit organizations relying on government funding, a debate has arisen surrounding AmeriCorps, which uses federal funds to pay "volunteers" to do work they might otherwise have performed without payment. In a reply to the previous article, also from *Policy Review*, Doug Bandow examines smaller organizations that see AmeriCorps not as promoting volunteerism, but instead as diverting potential volunteers away from long-term service in the private sector into short-term stints as government workers. Many still call attention to the fact that AmeriCorps is a program shared between government and nationwide volunteer groups. Bandow also questions whether this taxpayer-supported service will be worth its cost.

In Search of a Cause:
Volunteering Dos and Don'ts[1]

Rachel Levine wanted to help New York's homeless, so she went to the Mayor's Voluntary Action Center earlier this year looking for an organization to work with. She was referred to a women's shelter, where the volunteer coordinator welcomed her and told her to show up whenever she wished.

"They said I should just chat with the women," said Ms. Levine, 27, a budget and policy analyst in the Bronx Borough President's office. "There was no specific task. I'd rather have done something like serve a meal. I find it hard to make the connection if there's nothing to connect around."

This fall, during her first visit, Ms. Levine made labored conversation for an hour and a half and left. At her next visit, she did much the same, awkwardly asking the women how their dinner was. She is not planning to go back.

"It just didn't work for me," said Ms. Levine, who has now joined another volunteer organization, New York Cares, through which she spent a happy Saturday last month painting rooms in a hotel for formerly homeless people.

At a time when government is pulling in its safety net for the poor, urgent social needs are everywhere. At the Philadelphia summit on volunteerism last spring, President Clinton, acknowledging that government cannot solve all the nation's social ills, sought volunteers to help two million vulnerable children by the year 2000.

And many Americans want to help. While volunteering has waned slightly—in Independent Sector's latest survey, from 1995, 49 percent of adults reported volunteering, down from 54 percent in 1989—some 93 million Americans worked an average of four hours a week at churches, schools, hospitals, museums or, informally, an elderly neighbor's home.

But matching needs and good intentions is not simple. Many volunteers, like Ms. Levine, find some projects more satisfying than others. For example, Janet Zinn, a Manhattan therapist who for seven years delighted in feeding and cuddling babies in need through a St. Luke's Hospital program, dropped out after two visits to a soup kitchen. "While the infants taught me amazing, important lessons," Ms. Zinn said, the soup kitchen "felt like an obligation."

Even people who know what they like might have trouble finding their niche. Anaiza Castro Valle, a fashion assistant interested in art, and several like-minded friends wanted to run an art

---

[1] Article by Tamar Lewin, from the *New York Times* D 9 '97 G:2. Copyright © 1997 The New York Times. Reprinted with permission.

program for needy children, and even talked to a lawyer about setting up a nonprofit organization. "We wanted to do it at an orphanage, but we couldn't find one," Ms. Castro Valle said. "We called around, but no one could suggest an orphanage for us. Then I talked to a hospital, and they let us come in for a day."

But it was not what she hoped. "It was completely chaotic," Ms. Castro Valle said. "The children we worked with were emotionally unstable, due to their psychological problems. None of us were specialists in that, and we weren't well geared to children's behavior or emotional conflicts."

Like Ms. Levine, she then joined New York Cares, which is more flexible with volunteers and where Ms. Castro Valle now leads a children's art program at a family shelter. Volunteers attend an orientation, and receive a calendar of about 200 projects supervised by an experienced volunteer.

"Many social-service agencies cannot absorb a lot of untrained volunteers."

"This way, you get a lot of options, you know you're needed and you don't have to commit to being available every Thursday at 6:30," Kathleen Behrens, the director, said. "People have different reasons for volunteering and different levels of commitment and availability. But we have so many things that almost anybody who wants to help can find something that fits them."

For other organizations, though, good intentions may not be enough. Many social-service agencies cannot absorb a lot of untrained volunteers, and most put volunteers through vetting and training, especially if they intend to deal with children. Many require extended commitment.

"Around the holiday season, we get calls from people who look at their lives and think they should give of themselves," said Lyn Stone, the director of volunteers at the Jewish Guild for the Blind. "That's nice, but in January, they change their minds. We try to refer them to a one-time event, like serving a meal."

One promising approach to helping children, and one the Philadelphia summit called for expanding, is personal mentoring. In New York, Big Brothers/Big Sisters receives 4,000 calls a year from prospective mentors. But after learning that they must commit to seeing a child every other week for a year, only half show up for orientation. Another 1,000 drop out after that session. Half of the remaining 1,000 are eliminated in a screening process, where they are asked about their motivations, attitudes and social life, undergo a police check and personality profile and are asked for references from work, neighbors and friends.

"We have a waiting list of a thousand families, but you can't just throw Miss or Mr. X together with a kid and expect it to work," said Allan Luks, the executive director of the New York program. "When you add the ongoing supervision, it costs us $1,000 for each family we match. We know mentoring works, we know it's great for the kid and the volunteer. But we also know we don't have the staff or the money to multiply the number of families we serve."

Thy Neighbor's Keeper[2]

Ed Kirk says he's the "kind of person that doesn't believe in failure." A retired Bell Atlantic executive, Kirk lives in a Maryland suburb and has worshiped at Our Lady of the Fields Catholic Church for 20 years. Two years ago, he and his wife, Elaine, helped Jane, a 32-year-old single mom, get off welfare. (The names of former and current welfare recipients have been changed to protect their privacy.)

Every day for four months, Kirk rose before 7 a.m., picked up Jane and her toddler, dropped the boy off at the babysitter, and drove Jane to work. She did a lot of temping, and sometimes jobs were 30 or 40 miles away. During the long drives, he'd cheer and cajole.

"I was always talking to her positively, telling her she could get off welfare," Kirk says. He wouldn't let her dwell on the negative, tolerated no excuses for not working to resolve her problems, and encouraged her to focus on the future. After a 14-month roller coaster ride of hirings and firings, health problems, suspicious drug activity, eviction, and family reconciliation, Jane has finally settled into a full-time clerical job with medical benefits in Washington, D.C., and has her own apartment. Kirk says it's a success story but admits "it had a lot of bruises along the way."

Kirk's church is one of two dozen congregations in Maryland's Anne Arundel County that participate in the Community-Directed Assistance Program, or C-DAP. Launched in June 1994, the program links welfare recipients with small support teams of church volunteers. The church receives one year's worth of the recipient's AFDC benefits in a lump sum, and the volunteers and recipient work together for six months to tackle the obstacles to economic self-sufficiency and find stable, permanent employment. Since its inception, 21 welfare recipients have enrolled in C-DAP and 14 have not returned to the state's welfare rolls. Though small-scale, C-DAP is the most creative and thoughtfully constructed partnership between the religious community and local government I've seen while researching such initiatives in several states on the cutting edge of welfare reform. And soon more welfare recipients may be able to join something like C-DAP: Officials from Maryland's Frederick County and Washington County have invited C-DAP manager Remy Agee to teach them how to replicate the program.

Agee, an employee of Anne Arundel County's Department of Social Services, is quick to say that "C-DAP isn't for everyone." Because of its emphasis on work, pregnant welfare recipients or

[2] Article by Amy L. Sherman, director of urban ministry at Trinity Presbyterian Church, in Charlottesville, VA, and author of *Restorers of Hope: Reaching the Poor in Your Community with Church-Based Programs That Work* (Crossway), from *Reason* 29:43-6 Ag/S '97. Copyright © 1998 by the Reason Foundation, Los Angeles, CA. Reprinted with permission.

those with small children won't join. Recipients with drug problems are screened out, and recipients who want further schooling typically reject the offer to enroll in C-DAP. Furthermore, it appears that only churches are willing to make the long-term volunteer investment required of C-DAP mentors. Agee originally thought that service organizations, such as the Kiwanis or Rotary clubs, might be willing to help, but they turned her down. "They weren't willing to work as labor-intensively with a family for six months or more," she says.

While C-DAP is succeeding in helping recipients achieve independence from the dole, my study of 13 program participants shows the enormous difficulties of obtaining true self-sufficiency. "We and the public are learning," Agee reports, "that there are multiple issues for almost every family that is eligible for assistance. Most of the [C-DAP] participants have spiraled downward pretty far. They've exhausted their own resources and those of their families and friends." The relatively small number of C-DAP's success stories could lead one to question the initiative's value. Critics of welfare reform might argue that C-DAP's record proves that the challenge of moving needy families from dependence to self-sufficiency is just too great for private citizens; that only government with its large resources can handle it. In reality, though, the contrary is true. C-DAP provides a vivid and sobering reminder of why welfare reform was necessary. While the Maryland experiment counsels against an easy optimism about fixing the "underclass problem," it also demonstrates an innovative welfare-to-work approach that other states should consider imitating.

"The relatively small number of C-DAP's success stories could lead one to question the initiative's value."

With the devolution of welfare from Washington to the states, and from the states to civil society, governmental entities are stepping up their efforts to collaborate with private social service organizations, particularly churches and religious nonprofit groups. Mississippi Gov. Kirk Fordice's Faith and Families program aims to match every welfare family with a congregation that can help it achieve economic self-sufficiency. Gov. George Allen of Virginia has sponsored several regional conferences bringing together state bureaucrats, community nonprofits, and religious leaders to forge new alliances and facilitate welfare-to-work mentoring programs and new child care and job training initiatives. Govs. John Engler of Michigan and Parris Glendening of Maryland are taking similar steps.

Public partnerships with religious social service agencies aren't exactly novel. Stephen Monsma's recent study, *When Sacred and Secular Mix*, discusses hundreds of examples of cooperation between government and religious groups. Organizations like Catholic Charities and the Salvation Army make a huge impact serving the poor and receive considerable public funding. But the climate is new in two respects. First, the "charitable choice" provisions in the federal welfare reform law give religious social service groups that accept government funds explicit protections that enable them to carry out their work without compromising their unique religious identity and mission. Such protections make it more likely that evangelical Christian groups already fighting poverty will be able to expand their activities by accepting state money. Second, most previous collaboration was with religious nonprofits, not individual congregations. Aggressive attempts to stir churches to greater activity may provide a twofold blessing. They can harness previously untapped human and financial resources, and they can encourage a reformation of church benevolence: away from traditional, "commodity-based" outreach that gave poor people band-aids of money, food, and clothing, and toward "relationally based" service that addresses the root causes of persistent poverty and encourages permanent change.

The C-DAP model is a good one for churches and policy makers to consider for several reasons. First, it illustrates the ground-floor-up involvement critical to fruitful public-private collaboration. Agee, the C-DAP manager, held focus groups with business owners, community representatives, churches, and welfare recipients to shape a program that would address both the structural and the moral-cultural factors contributing to welfare dependence while drawing on the enormous human resources available in the religious community. Welfare recipients like Wanda, a 24-year-old mother of two, said they wanted more personalized assistance; they were "sick of being treated as faceless numbers by the [social services] bureaucracy." Businesses said they'd hire poor people if they had good attitudes and a personal support system to help them cope with the challenges of day care, transportation, and budgeting. Churches said they'd administer funds, teach money management, and provide caring volunteers—as long as they weren't matched with drug addicts and the county didn't smother them in red tape.

Agee and her colleagues listened, and created C-DAP from the grassroots up, rather than from the bureaucracy down. Too often, she admits, bureaucrats don't understand what's going on out in the community because they're not in field. "Every time we came back from a [focus group]," she says, "we changed the program, modifying it on the basis of that feedback."

Rather than issuing a vague plea for the churches to "adopt" welfare recipients, C-DAP personnel clearly define the program's expectations. Churches and C-DAP participants sign written agreements specifying the responsibilities of each. For example, churches are not to be approached for financial aid, and participants are the ones responsible for seeking employment. The volunteers' role is to "do with" the clients, not to "do for" them. Budget counseling is an important focus: Volunteers and C-DAP participants agree to develop a responsible spending plan immediately. The average participant, with three kids, gets a $4,200 allowance over six months (in addition to food stamps and other noncash subsidies).

Ed Kirk and other church volunteers report that most participants "needed a lot of education" when it came to finances.
"Some of the young mothers we've worked with didn't realize
they were spending 50 percent more than their income," comments a Methodist volunteer. He showed one participant how her
two phone lines, call waiting service, and deluxe cable TV pack-
age added a hefty burden to her monthly bills. Kirk remembers
taking Jane to the dry cleaner: "Cripes! She dropped off pleated
skirts, and it just about depleted her money for the whole week!"
Initially, C-DAP participant Tierra says she disliked the influence
the team had over the use of her money. "But I wasn't doing so
great a job," she admits. "I needed the help with budgeting."

Prior to the federal welfare reforms passed last fall, C-DAP was
financially front-loaded: The church had 12 months' worth of
funds to spend in six months. This made it possible for volunteers to tackle large, immediate barriers to employment. With
cash in hand, they could obtain expensive car repairs and so
enable participants to get to work; pay off debts that weighed
participants down; or get recipients' telephone service restored
so they could make and receive calls about jobs. Under the new
welfare rules, C-DAP participants will receive only six months'
worth of cash assistance for the six-month period.

*"In Mississippi,
churches
participating in
Faith and Families
have given their
'adoptees' grants
of up to $1,500."*

Sponsoring churches may be willing to contribute their own
money if C-DAP officials let them. This isn't a pipe dream:
Churches involved in northern Virginia's Project HOMES pay the
security deposits and first month's rent for the homeless families
they mentor, and congregations participating in the Tidewater
area's Partners in Hope project do the same for the battered
women they assist. In Mississippi, churches participating in Faith
and Families have given their "adoptees" grants of up to $1,500.

Another key to C-DAP's effectiveness is that it employs a team
approach rather than one-to-one mentoring. This cuts down on
volunteer burnout, increases the participants' network of con-
tacts, and allows volunteers to find their own niche. In the cases
I studied, usually one team member took on the role of day care
shopper, taking the participant around to different centers and
babysitters to find an affordable, convenient option. Others listened for job openings and coached participants on their interview skills, another helped with transportation, and another provided budget counseling.

C-DAP also supports volunteers by hosting occasional meetings
where teams from different churches gather to swap stories and
learn from each other's experiences. "That was extremely useful," says one volunteer. "In hearing from the other church volunteers, I realized we were too soft with our participant. You
don't want to pry. All the volunteers felt that. But then you realize that that's what you have to do." A man from a Catholic
church added that while his team had "tried to develop a good

rapport" with the participant through friendly, supportive conversation, sometimes it was necessary, though uncomfortable, to probe and "root out the problems," such as misplaced spending priorities or a disinclination to save. Knowing that other volunteers were doing this, and finding it effective, reassured him.

Finally, C-DAP personnel were prepared to play the heavy if a participant was not fulfilling her end of the bargain. Remy Agee would meet with her, review the original contract, discuss areas for improvement, and add specific action items to the agreement that the participant needed to complete by a deadline. "I'd tell them that this is a voluntary program and you don't have to be in it," Agee says. "But if you're going to be in it, then you've signed an agreement and you need to keep it."

According to C-DAP statistics, church volunteers spend an average of 400 hours with their participants over a six-month period. Some of the teams from the seven churches I surveyed had put in considerably more time—over 500 hours. "To get people back on their feet," Ed Kirk explains, "it's not just about getting a job. It's about getting all their problems solved." And Jane had a lot of problems. Her license had been revoked because of unpaid traffic fines. An acquaintance borrowed her car and wrecked it. She lived in an area not served by public transportation. The father of her son provided no assistance, and her family had written her off years before, when she'd gotten hooked on drugs.

"She owed money on her car loan," Kirk says. "She owed money to a hospital. She owed back state and federal taxes. Cripes! If they don't resolve each one of these problems, they're no better off than they were the day you met them." Most of these problems had to be handled during normal business hours, when Jane was working. So Kirk met with the bureaucrats, called the creditors, and drove to Washington to meet with the IRS, while his wife, Elaine, took Jane's toddler to the doctor if he got sick at the babysitter's. "It was a full-time job," Kirk says.

That reality points to the necessity for struggling individuals to re-affiliate with their families and seek aid from diverse sources. Recognizing the significant challenges Jane faced, Kirk encouraged her to contact her relatives and to begin attending a church near her home. Members of that church ended up providing a lot of free babysitting and transportation, thus easing the burden on the Kirks. To get her driver's license reinstated, Jane needed to pay traffic fines. So Kirk suggested that Jane call her father and explain that she was trying to make a fresh start in life. Her father paid half of the fines, while Jane used C-DAP funds for the other half. After some refresher driving lessons from Ed— and Jane's receipt of a donated used car through the county Department of Social Services—she was mobile once again. Several months after the Kirks began working with Jane, Jane's brother and sister-in-law also stepped forward and offered assistance.

Agee says this pattern is common. When weary family members see that their needy relative is receiving crucial emotional and personal support, they become more willing to help. They seem to have greater confidence that perhaps this time real change will occur.

Jane's bumpy ride to independence from welfare demonstrates clearly why reform was necessary. After all, if it's tough for a group of diligent, dedicated volunteers putting in many hours to help a person exit welfare, it's virtually impossible for a government caseworker, who doesn't have one-tenth the time, to help a client do so. "With their high caseload, [case] workers can provide only limited support," Agee observes. In my own county, according to Bryan Betts, management analyst for the Albemarle County, Virginia, Department of Social Services, a caseworker typically juggles 19 cases each month. County statistics indicate that caseworkers spend, on average, 6.5 hours a month on each case. The six-month total, then, is 39 hours dedicated to one welfare recipient—versus the 400 to 500 hours logged by the C-DAP volunteer teams.

"County statistics indicate that caseworkers spend, on average, 6.5 hours a month on each case."

And it's not just the quantity of time that is important. The quality of the relationship matters too. C-DAP participants said personal support made a huge difference. Last Mother's Day, Jane called Elaine Kirk and thanked her for "being like a mom." She also said that if Ed hadn't picked her up every day in those first few months, she would have skipped work. But she knew she had to get up and keep trying because he and Elaine were working so hard to help her. Now, many months later, Jane and the Kirks still keep in touch. "We'll never forget her," Elaine says, "and she says she'll never forget us."

Tierra, a stocky, feisty 37-year-old mother of three who's now in a manager-trainee program at a dry cleaning store, said she appreciated her team's "tough love." Somewhat unexpectedly, she reports, she clicked best with the volunteer who pushed her the hardest. "She was straight up, and I liked that," Tierra says with a smile. She confesses that she used to have a bad attitude that got in her way. I ask her what it takes to change someone's attitude. "Another person caring," she declares. "These are volunteers doing this. It's not a job. They care about you."

Some of the participants initially expressed concern that the team members might pressure them to join their church, but these fears never materialized. C-DAP staff told the churches that their involvement was not an opportunity for proselytizing. They really didn't have to, since church members saw their participation as community service, not missionary work. They invited participants to social events at the church, but, in the words of a Lutheran volunteer, "we did not press religion on our participant." Nearly all the volunteers were quiet about their faith, witnessing through deeds more than with words.

They didn't put their values on the shelf, however. They

expressed frustration when participants "didn't appreciate the urgency of getting to work on time or straightening out [their] finances," as volunteer Glenn Parker puts it. They expected participants to make meetings with them, keep job interview appointments, and stick to their budgets. Volunteers encouraged thrift, punctuality, showing respect on the job, sexual restraint, and personal responsibility. In short, they were willing to challenge self-destructive behavior or attitudes that hindered participants' progress. This was something the old welfare system rarely did, and really could not do very well, since it is best done in the context of a personal relationship of care, candor, and trust. C-DAP put welfare recipients into such friendships with caring individuals, who also took time to impart basic life skills—time management, keeping a checkbook, budgeting, smart shopping—essential to achieving and maintaining independence from public assistance.

C-DAP has many strengths. There's no bureaucratic inertia: The county's social services staff have modified the program as they've heard constructive criticism from front-line volunteers. Red tape is minimal. The volunteers often go beyond the call of duty. Taxpayer's money is spent carefully, in conjunction with a strategic plan for gaining stable, full-time employment. Welfare recipients are encouraged, treated with dignity, and given attentive, individually tailored assistance. Several have made remarkable progress in the face of overwhelming obstacles. As noted earlier, two-thirds of the C-DAP participants are now off the dole.

Still, if the real goal is genuine economic self-sufficiency rather than independence from cash aid, the statistics are a bit more sobering. By this criterion, only four of the 13 cases I examined were clear successes. Four others were clear failures and five were mixed. Such numbers force us to accept that even a good program—and C-DAP is very well conceived and managed—is no panacea. Ultimately, the individual recipient holds the key to success. As one volunteer put it, "All we can do is try to steer these people. If they don't really want to go, you can't force them." And some who do want to go lack the education, marketable skills, or reliable transportation needed to secure jobs with salaries that support two or three kids. Those with a good attitude and solid work ethic can move up over time, but without adequate transitional assistance such as day care subsidies and food stamps, they probably won't make it.

Fortunately, under the new welfare reforms many recipients will receive day care subsidies and medical assistance even after they are no longer eligible for cash aid. These measures address the "cliff effect" problem many C-DAP participants have encountered in the past. "We were really angry that as soon as [Donna] got a job, her rent went from $25 to $425 a month and she lost most of her food stamps," complained church volunteer Kathy McFadden. A Methodist volunteer agreed: "The clients need at least six months of earning a salary before they can even begin to take on some of the expenses that they're going to have to take on. The medical and day care assistance should continue for at least a year. We can't just cut them off and say, 'OK, now you're working, so you're no longer eligible for help.' They're not really self-sufficient yet."

Remy Agee enthusiastically reports that nine new churches are "ready and waiting" to be matched with C-DAP participants. Concurrent with the growing enthusiasm for C-DAP, though, is a disturbing rumbling in a segment of Maryland's religious community. A coalition claiming to represent 250 congregations recently met with Governor Glendening and told him they would not participate in "dehumanizing" welfare reforms, complaining that the government was abdicating its responsibilities and "dumping" the poor on the churches.

Agee says she's not really worried about this development, because she believes the coalition mainly opposes the state's "third party payee" idea. This proposal tries to address what happens when a parent is kicked off the welfare rolls because of noncompliance with the new rules, such as work requirements. To ensure that such children continue to receive the aid they need, the state wants churches to administer the kids' cash aid and food stamps. Agee says that program is distinct from the C-DAP initiative, so the coalition's activities won't hamper C-DAP's growth.

Religious leaders in other states have also been critical of welfare reform, but this need not hinder a new engagement of churches in this era of welfare devolution. While the denominational headquarters may be crying foul, many average pew sitters are not. John Wells, director of a network of mainline churches in Virginia called Community Ministries, reports that what he hears from local pastors contradicts the official messages articulated by denominational leaders. "The Spirit is not very alive in many of our churches, and the preachers know it," he says candidly. "They are hungry for opportunities to put in front of their members opportunities to get personally involved in ministry." Wells criticizes national religious leaders whose emphasis on mobilizing parishioners in partisan lobbying efforts distracts the laity from a humble, hands-on service that can deepen their faith.

The Washington Post reported on the Maryland coalition's stormy meeting with Glendening just a few days before I interviewed Dot and Annette, C-DAP volunteers from the Severna Park United Methodist Church. They were exasperated by the coalition's attitude. Rather than disavowing its duty, they argued, the church should be stepping up its efforts. "We've been critical of welfare before because it didn't seem to be helping people," says Dot. Now that it's changed, she reasons, "we've got to put our actions where our mouths are."

The Smart Samaritan[3]

Government programs of social assistance are on the wane. They still enjoy enormous political and budgetary clout, but they are losing intellectual and moral support. Voters are clamoring for retrenchment, and policymakers are pondering ways—such as tax credits and government grants and contracts—to create a larger role for private organizations in the welfare system. President Clinton, announcing a national summit on volunteerism to be held in April, said, "Much of the work of America cannot be done by government. The solution must be the American people through voluntary service to others." The future of social assistance, it appears, will be in the hands of nonprofits, churches, and volunteer groups.

"The government system has failed because it has followed a defective approach to helping the poor."

This transformation will not, however, automatically create a better welfare system. The government system has failed because it has followed a defective approach to helping the poor. If the private sector maintains that approach—and it is in danger of doing so—we could end up with a welfare regime just as dysfunctional as the one we are struggling to replace. Before the country plunges into the brave new world of voluntary charity, we need to do some hard thinking about the right way and wrong way to give assistance to the needy. Here are some principles that charity leaders and volunteers ought to consider as they devise their own programs.

1. Unexamined giving leads to defective charity.

Upon seeing a needy person, a benefactor's first impulse is a desire to fill the need. We see a beggar on the street who seems hungry, and we give him food. We see a person who is homeless, and we give him shelter. This is "sympathetic giving": giving according to the sympathy or pity one feels for the plight of the needy person. The problem is that such giving tends to "reward" the plight: Instead of lifting the recipient to self-sufficiency, sympathetic giving reinforces his bad habits and undercuts his motivation to reform himself. In this way, it leads to dependency and an ever-growing demand for more giving.

Government programs are typically programs of sympathetic giving. Although they are sold to the public as a "hand up," they are—or almost invariably become—"handouts," that is, giveaways of goods and services based on the apparent need of the recipients. Hence, the programs inadvertently reinforce bad habits and wrong choices: losing a job because of drug or alcohol abuse, dropping out of school, not saving money, having children one cannot support, not striving to overcome a disabil-

---

[3] Article by James L. Payne, a 1996 Bradley Fellow at the Heritage Foundation, editor of *The Befriending Leader: Social Assistance Without Dependency* (Lytton), from *Policy Review* 83:48-53 My/Je '97. Copyright © 1997 *Policy Review*. Reprinted with permission.

ity, and so on.

Modern charity workers and donors need a comprehensive theory of giving to replace this flawed doctrine. Fortunately, we do not need to invent it. The 19th-century charity theorists covered this ground thoroughly, and they have left us a clear account of their conclusions.

Earlier reformers insisted that sound policy requires more than pity toward the needy. It must also include tough-minded analysis. In 1876, American preacher and sociologist Charles Ames put it this way:

"The open hand must be guided by the open eye. The impulse of pity, or compassion for suffering, belongs to every well-ordered mind; but like every other impulse, taken by itself alone, it is blind and idiotic. Unable to protect itself against imposition, unable also to discriminate and adapt its relief to the various conditions of actual helplessness, it flings its resources abroad at haphazard, and gushes itself to death."

In many private charities around the country, this advice is disregarded. All too often, charity volunteers assume that if they are motivated by compassion, there is no reason to examine the long-term effect of their programs.

In Sacramento, California, a group of reformers started a homeless shelter in 1983 called Loaves and Fishes. The philosophy is pure sympathetic giving. As a staff member told me, "We have no requirements, no expectations. We don't expect people to be in treatment programs or attend certain meetings in order to be fed and to receive services here."

They have worked hard to give homeless people material things to make their lives easier. In addition to giving them morning coffee and a full-course lunch every day, the shelter provides them with free medical care, a library and reading room, free locker storage, free kennel service and veterinary care for their dogs, free pet food, free ice, a bank of free telephones, whist and bridge tables, horseshoes, basketball, and soft drink machines. Members of the staff are careful not to judge or criticize the lifestyle of those being helped, whom they call "guests." Nowhere have they posted advice or exhortation to improve behavior. There are no mottos over doorways, no Bible verses on bulletin boards, no posters urging people to get off drugs.

Not surprisingly, all these benefits and facilities lead to increased demand, even in good economic times. Now feeding nearly 1,000 people a day, Loaves and Fishes is attempting its third expansion—and is being opposed by many local residents who fear the open-ended growth of homelessness that the shelter is encouraging.

Many churches establish assistance programs like soup kitchens without exploring what anyone wants to achieve with this activity. Do volunteers want clients to depend permanently on the soup kitchen? Do they want recipients to get jobs? To learn good nutrition? To learn how to cook? To learn manners?

To help run the kitchen? To experience spiritual growth? Until all these issues are carefully addressed, it is not possible to know how to operate a truly constructive program.

Several traditions underlie the failure to analyze the consequences of giving. For one thing, government welfare programs have given us a century-long example of thoughtless giving. Highly trained professional social workers have participated in and endorsed this vast system of handouts; who are we, say the ladies of the soup kitchen, to question the practice of blind giving, of giving without expecting anything in return?

Sometimes, misguided religious impulses are the culprit. Sharon M. Daly, the deputy director for social policy at Catholic Charities USA, declares that "the primary purpose of charity is not to reform the poor, but to bring us closer to God—to save our own souls." This view of giving is self-centered, downplaying the importance of finding out whether our gifts to the poor are really beneficent.

At my home church in Sandpoint, Idaho, I came upon a volunteer, a kind and worthy woman, distributing plastic bags to parishioners for a food drive. I asked her if she knew whether the food would actually help the people who would get it. She frankly confessed to having made no effort to find out who received the food, or why, or how it might affect their lives for good or ill. "That's not my job," she said. "All I know is I tried; my conscience is clear."

Religiously based self-sacrifice may be admirable, but it should not be carried on at the expense of the poor. If we say we care about the poor, then it is our duty to help *them*. We must shift attention from ourselves, as givers, to those we try to help.

"We must shift attention from ourselves, as givers, to those we try to help."

2. Real charity attaches expectations to assistance.

Sympathetic giving is not the only approach to the problems of the needy. There is an alternative method: giving in exchange for some contribution or achievement of the recipient. This can be called "expectant giving," since the donor has something in mind that he expects from the recipient in return for the aid. The obvious example is work. When a beggar says he is hungry, the donor doesn't just give food; he asks for useful labor in exchange.

Expectant giving takes many forms, from simple exchanges of material things to subtle psychological transactions. For example, a healthy teacher-student relationship involves expectant giving: the teacher makes an effort to motivate and instruct the pupil, who is expected to work hard to master the material. The 19th-century charity leaders discovered expectant giving and made it the key to uplift. Homeless men who wanted shelter had to chop wood for several hours; unwed mothers in charity homes had to follow a strict regimen of training and domestic duties.

Modern charities are beginning to rediscover this principle. For example, many private programs that provide transitional housing for the homeless now require a self-help contract in which the client agrees to stay employed, save money, keep his quarters neat, and so on. Even government is attempting to embrace the exchange idea by putting work requirements in a few of its benefits programs. (Unfortunately, these have a tendency to be watered down or ignored as the program matures.)

Giveaways, then, are never "the best we can do." Even with slender resources, it is possible to create constructive programs of expectant giving, programs about which staff members, volunteers, and donors will feel enthusiastic. The giveaway approach is a warning sign of a lack of imagination, or a burnt-out staff, or volunteers held at arm's length from the people they serve, or an agency comfortably dependent on government subsidies. They almost certainly signify that leaders are not holding monthly meetings about the purpose of the program and whether it is really helping its clients.

Those who defend programs based on sympathetic giving—governmental and private—often claim that the giveaway is "better than nothing." The point cannot be conceded. The general effect of sympathetic giving is to enhance the viability of a dysfunctional—and therefore suffering—lifestyle.

There are exceptions, but sympathetic giving is generally harmful to recipients. This is the general principle that all the 19th-century charity theorists divined. This old truth may disturb us, but the path to sound policy requires that we grasp it. The routinized, unconditional giving of material assistance to strangers has to be seen as a *vice*—yes, a destructive impulse—not a praise-worthy activity.

Unfortunately, handouts have become so widespread that we take them for granted. In giving out medical care, for example, government never asks for any contributions or repayment. Private charitable clinics show that it doesn't have to be this way. At the East Liberty Family Health Care Center, in Pittsburgh, Pennsylvania, the staff practices "fee counseling." The bookkeeper meets with the client, explains the full cost of the service, and points out that the client has a responsibility to repay as much as he is able, within his means, and a payment plan is worked out. No proof of income or assets is required. Clinic staff report an extremely high level of compliance with these voluntary payment plans.

The Lawndale Christian Health Center in Chicago charges a minimal fee of $8 per visit, with a sliding scale of payment based on family size and income. For clients with no money, says co-founder Wayne Gordon, "we have a long list of jobs that need to be done." This is healthier all around. "The truth is that most people want to work. They want to give something in return for what they have received."

Sometimes, a giveaway program may offer no useful way to implement this notion of exchange. That's a revealing piece of information. It suggests that given its resources, expertise, and clientele, the group is operating in unpromising territory. It should shift to a helping program where it *can* effect an exchange. For example, a group of middle-class women running a food bank for inner-city drug addicts may find that charging for the food, or requiring work in exchange, means that there will be no clients. The conclusion should not be that a giveaway is "the best we can do." It should be that "we're out of our depth." They should turn their energies to an activity better suited to their talents and resources—perhaps organizing a baby-sitting club for low-income mothers.

3. Mentoring is the foundation of uplift.

In a materialistic age, we assume that money can buy anything, including the uplift of the needy. After spending many trillions of dollars, we are beginning to sense the inadequacy of this assumption. Material support may have a role to play in certain types of assistance, but it is not an engine of uplift. For most people deemed needy, the main barrier to economic and social success is not a lack of dollar bills; it is a lack of healthy values and motives. We need to teach children—and adults—to work hard, to spend their money wisely, to be honest, to stay away from drugs and alcohol. We need, in short, mentors—individuals who befriend, guide, and inspire the needy.

"Mentoring is a complex, subtle task involving many emotional and intellectual factors."

Mentoring is a complex, subtle task involving many emotional and intellectual factors. Government welfare systems have ignored it because its emphasis on personal relationships clashes with the needs of bureaucracy, and because it doesn't have material inputs and outputs that social engineers can measure and manage. For the charity workers of the 19th century, however, mentoring—called "friendly visiting"—was the primary technique of social assistance.

Seeing that it was crucial to get mentors into regular, businesslike contact with their charges, British charity worker Octavia Hill set up a system of housing management in which middle-class ladies served as managers and rent collectors in low-income housing projects. She explained her theory of mentoring in an 1880 letter:

"From wealth, little can be hoped; from intercourse, everything. That is to say, everything we have to give seems to communicate itself to those we love and know; if we are true, we make them truthful, if faithful, full of faith, if earnest and energetic, earnest and energetic.... Human intercourse in God's own mercy seems appointed to be the influence strongest of all for molding character."

Modern-day Octavia Hills have come forth in recent years to apply this old idea of putting helpers and helped into personal contact. In 1976, Virgil Gulker developed a program in Holland, Michigan, to put individual church members in contact with people who needed their skills and support. Gulker devised the system after he discovered that church members were being cut off from the needy. In his book *Help Is Just Around the Corner*,

Gulker explains the problem: "The usual arrangements for help-ing the needy remove opportunities from church members, reserving those opportunities for a corps of professionals.... Church members are deprived of their privilege, their birthright, to minister 'to the least of these.'"

Moreover, Gulker says, too many assistance efforts focused exclusively on meeting people's physical needs: "We made it vir-tually impossible for them to achieve any level of self-esteem, because the helping experience was not designed to give them the help they really needed to become self-sufficient." Gulker's system for involving people in a direct personal way with those who need assistance—called Love, Inc.—has since spread to 102 towns in 39 states.

4. Helpers should feel proud of their clients.

All too often, social assistance is seen as a "sacrificing" activity, something unpleasant done out of a sense of obligation. Duty has its place in charity, but mainly as a spark plug, a motive for getting involved initially. In the long run, it is not a healthy drive, and it will not lead to a successful social-assistance program.

Once again, Octavia Hill illustrates the ideal. As her writings make clear, she took enormous delight in her activities as a vol-unteer apartment manager, and had great pride in her tenants. If helpers don't feel rewarded and enthusiastic about their clients, it is a sign that these clients are simply not being uplifted.

One of the most common sources of discouragement among staff members and volunteers is their involvement in a program of sympathetic giving. Helpers sense that they are only treating symptoms and not providing lasting help. And since clients aren't being uplifted, helpers find little to admire about them.

This point comes out clearly in *Tell Them Who I Am*, Elliot Liebow's in-depth account of several homeless shelters in the Washington, D.C., area. These shelters were run on the giveaway principle, with no significant effort expected from clients. Liebow was distressed to discover that many volunteers and staff mem-bers privately resented those receiving assistance. He recounts an incident in which several men at a soup kitchen complained that their soup wasn't hot. When Liebow took the bowls back to the volunteer serving the soup, she refused to reheat it. He brought the matter to the attention of the assistant manager, and was also rebuffed. "I don't know what they're complaining about," the assistant manager said. "This ain't the Waldorf Astoria, and they're getting it for free."

When a client at a women's shelter refused tuna casserole and asked for something different, a volunteer privately shared her frustration with Liebow: "Those seven people who were killed last week [the Challenger astronauts]—they gave so much to the world, and they died giving more. But these people, they give nothing. All they do is take and take and ask for more."

Although staff members and volunteers thought they were hid-ing their resentment, Liebow found that clients often sensed it, and, of course, were hurt. The overall result was tragically ironic. Volunteers and staffers wanted to help the homeless, but because their giveaway programs put clients in a bad light, the volunteers disparaged them and unintentionally impaired the clients' already fragile self-esteem. The situation resembles a family in which the parents don't demand that their children contribute to the household. The parents start to resent them for being lazy and selfish, which in turn makes the children insecure.

While visiting charities around the country, I have been struck by the correlation between the type of giving and the enthusiasm of workers and volunteers. In charities that run giveaway programs, participants tend to be weary and frustrated—and also rather secretive. They are often unwilling to talk about the program they serve. On the other hand, morale is high in programs that demand a great deal from clients. Staff members are so enthusiastic about such programs that they won't let an interview end.

5. Economic opportunity is the key to long-term independence.

When charity reformers gather for their discussions of strategies and purposes, they should avoid focusing on the things needy people may lack. Their plan may involve material assistance, but the thrust of their efforts should be on creating opportunities that let people fill their own needs. "I believe we can solve the problem of homelessness," says John Woods, a former executive director of the Gospel Mission of Washington, D.C. "But we need to stop asking what we can do for the homeless. The success of a homeless program hinges on what it enables the homeless to accomplish on their own."

Nearly everyone agrees that the opportunities the poor need most are jobs—not government work programs, but meaningful, economically justified work. A job is the greatest anti-poverty device known, for it serves three uplifting functions all at once: It provides income, it builds self-esteem, and it cultivates constructive personal habits like behaving responsibly and getting along with others.

Suppose that we are members of a reform group that has recognized this vital point. We decide that we want to engage in a job-creation program. We begin to explore the kind of business our charity organization should start. A landscaping firm that will help beautify the town? A restaurant that will serve low-income customers? A day-care center? Members are assigned to research these possibilities.

At the next meeting, they return with a somber picture. Yes, the poor do need jobs in these kinds of businesses, and yes, the services they would provide the community would be valuable. But running a business is a difficult challenge. It takes someone enormously dedicated and persistent, willing to put in long hours,

"In charities that run giveaway programs, participants tend to be weary and frustrated—and also rather secretive."

someone who knows the technology, the market, and the suppliers, someone who knows how to motivate and discipline a work force. Our charity organization, say the researchers, has no one with this kind of expertise and commitment. If we tried to run the business ourselves, it would probably crash, throwing all the workers we intended to help out on the street.

At this point, many civic groups would give up on this idea and look for an easier, less demanding way to help the poor. But in so doing they ignore an astonishing fact: Although volunteers at most charities are not job-creation specialists, millions of Americans are. They already run millions of small businesses, including landscaping firms, restaurants, and day-care centers. The solution is obvious: Instead of trying to reinvent the wheel, why not assist small businesses that already help the poor with both jobs and needed services?

What kind of services might be provided? Some answers come from organizations that have already gone into the business of helping business. In Milwaukee, the farsighted Community Baptist Church started a business development center in 1987 called the Community Enterprises of Greater Milwaukee. Its staff and volunteers help entrepreneurs develop their ideas, put them in contact with credit sources, and also lease space where start-up businesses can operate. Director Bill Lock reports that in the past eight years, the organization has helped 11 businesses, including a firm that provides elderly in-home support, a sheet-metal company, and an electrical-products distribution company founded by a former welfare recipient.

Another way reformers can help small business is by providing loans. Ideally, the loans become a method of establishing personal relationships with owners, managers, and employees, so that charity workers can help businesses in many informal ways. They could be mentors, for example, encouraging wise business practices. They might also serve as peacemakers. Employer-employee relationships in small businesses are often stormy; mediators are needed to patch up disputes that hurt everyone.

Helping the poor in the 21st century will require us to profoundly rethink our theories of social assistance. For the past century, reformers have regarded business as the natural enemy of the poor, and government as their natural savior. We are now beginning to discern that both impulses were tragically misguided. Business is not the foe of the poor but the provider of the jobs, goods, and services they need to make their way up in the world. And government, with its indiscriminate dole and cynical regulations, is no ally of the poor. The next century of reform will turn the old models upside down, as reformers find ways to help business help the poor, and work to get government out of the way.

THINKING ABOUT GIVING

A suburban Washington church runs an assistance program for the homeless of the District of Columbia, giving them food, clothing, travel vouchers, and small amounts of cash. I asked one staff member, a social worker of wide experience with street people, what percentage of the clients of this program were either alcoholics or drug addicted. "Ninety-eight percent," she replied. She went on to explain how these clients were obviously in need of counseling, befriending, and inspiring—if anything at all could reach them—and that food and clothing were essentially irrelevant to their real needs.

Toward the end of the interview, an elderly middle-class volunteer came into the room bearing a carton of juice packets she was donating to the program. I asked her the same question about the percentage of clients who were drug- and alcohol-addicted. "Oh, I would say 10 percent," was her reply. Clearly, someone is seriously misinformed about the clientele being served by this program. Perhaps it is the volunteer, perhaps it is the social worker. The important point is that issues like this must be raised before any program can supply effective assistance.

Every social assistance program needs an analytical component. Staff, board members, volunteers, and donors need to gather frequently to analyze goals and methods. Groups should have a one-hour meeting at least once a month devoted exclusively to this function. Questions to be discussed at such meetings should include the following:

1. Who are our recipients and how should our program help them?

2. How do we know we are helping them?

3. In what way might our program be harming recipients (or others)?

4. How can we bring about more direct personal contact between helpers and helped?

Renewing the Call to Service[4]

Just when it seemed that a long, chilling winter of cynicism and partisan bickering had descended upon American public life, a few sprigs of green have popped up. A single flower doth not a springtime make, but the emerging story of what is occurring in the field of national service gives hope that perhaps one day—after this election season?—we may find our way back to civility.

The story has its roots in the time of George Bush. Disillusioned with the welfare state, the former president came to believe that a vibrant spirit of volunteerism might serve as a worthy replacement, so he launched his thousand Points of Light. Under the direction of an able assistant, Gregg Petersmeyer, the program could soon claim a string of modest but inspiring successes across the country. As he was leaving office, Bush told his successor, Bill Clinton, that he had only one personal request: the preservation and strengthening of Points of Light.

"For a time this year, it appeared that both AmeriCorps and the Points of Light Foundation might collapse."

Sadly, the Clinton team couldn't have cared less. Instead, the new president proposed his own, more expensive project—a domestic Peace Corps—and his Democratic allies on Capitol Hill began mocking the Bush approach with a thousand points of ridicule. Silly, meaningless, a thinly disguised retreat from government responsibility, they said of the Bush initiative. Not surprisingly, many Republicans took umbrage. And sure enough, by the time the Clinton initiative—called AmeriCorps—was up and running, the GOP pummeled it with criticism. A thinly disguised extension of the welfare state, sniffed Newt Gingrich. For a time this year, it appeared that both AmeriCorps and the Points of Light Foundation might collapse.

Enter Harris Wofford. A civil rights adviser to President Kennedy, an early leader of the Peace Corps and a former president of Bryn Mawr, Wofford was recovering from a Senate election defeat when Clinton asked him to run the umbrella organization for all federally funded volunteer and service programs.

In past months, Wofford and his team set out to rescue AmeriCorps as well as Points of Light by rebuilding a foundation of bipartisan support for national service. With one hand, they negotiated changes in AmeriCorps demanded by Republicans, led by Sen. Charles Grassley of Iowa. In successful budget talks, Wofford even insisted on more spending for Points of Light as he was accepting fewer funds for AmeriCorps. With the other hand, Wofford reached out to Bush and Petersmeyer, enlisting their help in seeking new ways to expand volunteerism and full-time service. Watch for more cooperation in coming months.

---

[4] Article by David Gergen from *U.S. News & World Report* 120:26+ My 20 '96. Copyright © 1996 *U.S. News & World Report*. Reprinted with permission.

If the presidential campaigns will now resist the temptation to play politics with national service, this coming together could serve as a springboard for a dramatic, much-needed breakthrough. Across the country, one finds a huge, growing hunger among Americans to find more meaning in life—through spirituality, service or both. Many different groups tap into that desire for service, from federally run efforts such as VISTA and the Retired and Senior Volunteer Program (RSVP) to religiously inspired ones such as the Jesuit and Lutheran corps. On campuses, far more students are working in mental hospitals, schools and soup kitchens than in the activist '60s, while older Americans are also lining up as volunteers.

The problem is that the country doesn't offer enough good opportunities for those who want to serve full time for a year or more. The Peace Corps accepts only 1 out of 3 who apply, and Teach for America turns away 5 applicants for every 1 it accepts. Nor does our culture celebrate service the way we should. In too many graduate admissions offices, a two-year stint on Wall Street counts far more than two years on an urban Main Street.

Wofford believes that America could "crack the atom" if we could link national service to a national strategy for addressing deep-seated social needs such as better schools, curbing crime and drugs, and reducing homelessness. "The trends of government downsizing and growing social problems make the work of volunteer engagement more important than ever before," says Wofford. He's right—just as George Bush was. If we elevate service to a more exalted place in our national life, those answering the call could one day make Americans feel we all belong to the same family...again.

"Across the country, one finds a huge, growing hunger among Americans to find more meaning in life—through spirituality, service, or both."

AmeriCorps the Beautiful?
Habitat for Conservative Values[5]

Let's conduct what Charles Murray might call "a thought experiment." Imagine it's 1993 and Newt Gingrich has been sworn in as president. In his Inaugural Address, he pledges to "dismantle the welfare state and replace it with an Opportunity Society." He appoints a task force of the party's most creative conservatives to ensure that citizen action will fill the void left by the withdrawal of government.

There is, by no means, unanimity. The Cato Institute's Doug Bandow argues that as government recedes, charities and volunteer groups will naturally fill the gap. Arianna Huffington says that the nonprofit sector must become more effective and less bureaucratic. Gingrich agrees and advises the task force to look at Habitat for Humanity as a model for truly effective compassion—inexpensive, nongovernmental, and faith-based.

From Switzerland, William F. Buckley Jr. faxes in a chapter from his book *Gratitude* calling for a national-service program to engage young people in solving problems outside of government bureaucracies. Jim Pinkerton urges the re-creation of the Civilian Conservation Corps on a massive scale. Colin Powell reminds the group that the most successful race- and class-mixing program has not been busing or quotas but service in the U.S. Army.

William Bennett argues that all government benefits ought to require something of the beneficiaries in turn, shattering the entitlement mentality created by years of Democrat-created welfare programs. Senator Dan Coats suggests that government's role should be confined to helping local community-based institutions solve their own problems.

The task force decides unanimously that there should be no big federal program, with armies of Washington bureaucrats telling communities what to do. Instead, Washington would give money to states to help local community groups help themselves.

And, inspired by Buckley, the members of the task force hit on an innovative idea. Instead of just giving grants to nonprofit groups, thereby creating nonprofit bureaucracies, they could model it after programs like the Jesuit Volunteer Corps, to which committed young people devote themselves for a year or two of service. The federal government would in turn provide that young person with a "service scholarship." This would, someone points out, establish a principle that the "educrats" in the higher-education lobby have always opposed: financial aid awarded not on need but merit, merit in this case defined as a willingness

---

[5] Article by Harris Wofford, former Democratic senator from Pennsylvania, now the CEO of the Corporation for National Service, and Steven Waldman, senior advisor for policy, planning and evaluation and the author of *The Bill*, a book about AmeriCorps; from *Policy Review* 79:28-36 S/O '96. Copyright © 1996 *Policy Review*. Reprinted with permission.

to serve one's country.

Pollster Frank Luntz tells Gingrich that even though it's a decentralized, community-based program, the young people it engages should be linked together with a national spirit—and name. Haley Barbour suggests "RepubliCorps" but Gingrich believes that might deprive it of bipartisan support. He asks his advisors to come up with a better name and gives them one bit of advice, "Don't be afraid to make it sound patriotic. Unlike the other party, we are not embarrassed to be Americans." So Luntz has a brainstorm: Let's call it "AmeriCorps."

The reality, of course, is that Bill Clinton thought of AmeriCorps first, and most Washington Republicans ended up opposing it as typical Big-Government liberalism. Republicans in Congress are now on the wrong side not only of the politics—AmeriCorps is popular with voters—but of their own ideology.

There is, however, a striking difference between the comments of Beltway Republicans and those in the rest of the country. New Hampshire governor Steve Merrill has called AmeriCorps "a great success in the state of New Hampshire." Michigan governor John Engler has said AmeriCorps "captures the promise found in all citizens." Arizona governor Fife Symington said he was "enthusiastic and impressed with the work of AmeriCorps." And Massachusetts governor William Weld called it "one of the most intelligent uses of taxpayer money ever." Let us explain why we think these Republican governors are right.

Readers of *Policy Review* will not need much persuading that government cannot solve many of our problems. But just as liberals have to be more realistic about the limits of government, conservatives need to be more realistic about the limits of the volunteer sector. One of the most common criticisms of AmeriCorps is that it is not needed in a nation in which 90 million people are volunteering. That is a weak argument.

First, one-third of the volunteering done by those 90 million Americans consists of serving on committees, baby-sitting, singing in the church choir, or other activities that are beneficial but hardly a substitute for the welfare state. Second, while the potential power of the volunteer sector is awesome, the trend is in the wrong direction. Just as a social consensus against government solutions has begun to emerge, Americans have been volunteering *less*, according to estimates by the Independent Sector.

As women have moved into the labor market, the composition of the volunteer force has changed. Most people now are free only on weekends or evenings. That limits the types of volunteer work they can perform. Most important, harnessing the power of volunteers is not easy. Volunteers need to be trained, supervised, and deployed well to be effective. As former Michigan governor George Romney said, "There is no free lunch when it comes to volunteering."

Some conservatives argue that even if the charitable sector has limits, governmental solutions will only make matters worse.

"Paying" AmeriCorps members, the argument goes, subverts the idea of volunteerism—labor given for love, not money. In an article for the January-February 1996 issue of *Policy Review*, John Walters of the New Citizenship Project argued that AmeriCorps's "very premise—using federal resources to promote voluntarism—contradicts the principle of self-government that lies at the heart of citizenship." Paid volunteerism, he wrote, would sap the strength of the nonprofit sector at precisely the moment when it most needs to flourish.

This argument ignores the experience of the past two years. Many of America's most respected nonprofits, from Big Brothers/Big Sisters to the YMCA to the American Red Cross, participate in and staunchly support AmeriCorps. A year ago, leaders of 24 volunteer groups wrote that AmeriCorps is an "enormously beneficial addition to the traditional voluntary sector. This program has not undermined our position, rather it has enhanced our efforts and strengthened our institutions."

"Many of America's most respected nonprofits... participate in and staunchly support AmeriCorps."

To understand why, consider the case of Habitat for Humanity, one of the most successful faith-based volunteer groups. The founder, Millard Fuller, was wary of any involvement with AmeriCorps precisely because he feared a government program would distort the religious nature of his effort. But on the urging of his board, Habitat brought in some AmeriCorps members.

Fuller used AmeriCorps to solve a particular problem. Habitat was flooded with good people who wanted to help build houses but didn't have enough full-time crew leaders to organize the volunteers. They selected AmeriCorps applicants who they thought might help. These full-time AmeriCorps members dramatically increased the number and effectiveness of the unpaid volunteers. In Miami, for instance, two dozen Habitat-AmeriCorps members coordinated, organized, trained, and worked alongside about 5,000 unpaid volunteers, who together built 50 homes in a little more than a year.

Now Fuller is a fan. "As AmeriCorps members gain in construction skill," he says, "our affiliates are able to expand the number of occasional volunteers through increased capacity to supervise and manage volunteers. We at Habitat for Humanity feel privileged and honored to have AmeriCorps people with us, and we want more of them."

Habitat's experience is instructive, not only because it is Newt Gingrich's favorite charity, but because it is a faith-based organization that did not have to alter its spiritual mission to make use of AmeriCorps members. This has been the experience of all the religious groups—from the nuns of the Notre Dame de Namur mission to the Greater Dallas Community Churches—that have brought on AmeriCorps members. The reason for their confidence is simple: *they* choose the AmeriCorps members, *they* train them, and if they're not working out, *they* send them home.

The Habitat story is not unusual. One independent study has found that each AmeriCorps member has "leveraged" 12 unstipended volunteers. It was a recognition that volunteer groups need a cadre of full-time people to organize volunteers that led George Romney to refer to full-time stipended service and unpaid volunteers as the "twin engines of service."

Even if one accepts the idea that volunteers need to be organized, why not just give the money to the nonprofit to hire its own full-time staff person? Because charities are quite capable of becoming bureaucratic. We need an infusion of people who plan to work only a year or two and have not, therefore, developed a careerist mindset. Besides, AmeriCorps members are much cheaper than full-time staff.

Service programs also provide a nonbureaucratic alternative to traditional government. One of the reasons the Peace Corps has enjoyed bipartisan support is that the money funds volunteers directly. Someday conservatives will view domestic national service as the antidote to bureaucracy.

Consider what AmeriCorps members have accomplished in rural, impoverished Simpson County, Kentucky. Over nine months of service in 1995, 122 second-graders served by 25 AmeriCorps members saw their reading comprehension scores improve by more than three grade levels. Thirty-seven percent improved by four or more grade levels. The reasons for success are quite simple. AmeriCorps volunteers can develop intense, one-on-one tutoring relationships and become familiar with the academic and emotional problems of the child. Just as important, AmeriCorps members visit each student's home every other week to show parents their child's classroom materials and suggest ways for them to help. Parental involvement has increased dramatically. Would this have happened if the federal government had given the grant to the state education agency?

Simply put, the nonprofits that use AmeriCorps members can provide services more efficiently, humanely, and cost-effectively than government can.

There has been a great deal of confusion about the costs of AmeriCorps. The standard AmeriCorps living allowance is $7,945—about $160 a week—of which $6,700 comes from the federal government. Those members with no health insurance also get a health plan valued at $1,200. So direct compensation is just more than $9,000. If they finish a year of service, they get a $4,725 scholarship.

On top of that, the Corporation for National Service gives grants to local programs to help manage the AmeriCorps members. If the program builds low-income housing, that might include the cost of supplies. If the program establishes crew-based corps, that might include the cost of supervising them. If the corps helps a disaster-struck area, this would include travel costs. Then there are the administrative costs, which are distributed between the headquarters staff and the governor-appointed state commissions that distribute much of the money. The total cost to the Corporation per AmeriCorps member averages $18,800.

Programs are encouraged to raise outside money to supplement that provided by the federal government. Indeed, they can choose to add extra training, supplies, or supervision if they feel that enriches the quality—but only if they raise the money from somewhere else.

At first blush, $18,000 "per corps member" sounds like a lot of money. But think about it. This is direct compensation plus all the other costs associated with the program. If you used the same calculus for Microsoft Corp.—the total budget divided by the number of employees—the average "cost per employee" would be about $150,000.

It's easy to see that this methodology has limited value, for it doesn't tell what you are getting for your money. We know what "benefit" or "product" the Microsoft investment produces. The truth is $18,000 could be a lousy deal—or a real bargain—depending on what the AmeriCorps members do.

AmeriCorps members help solve problems. According to partial results from a study by Aguirre Associates, an independent consulting firm, 1,353 AmeriCorps members in 12 states restored 24 beaches, enhanced 338 miles of river banks, planted 200,000 trees, constructed 440 dams, and cleaned up 139 neighborhoods. In all, they estimated these Corps members working on environmental issues in those states "affected the lives" of 469,000 people.

Three separate independent evaluations of the cost-benefit ratio of the program predict measurable returns between $1.54 and $2.60 for every AmeriCorps dollar invested. Each study concluded that AmeriCorps's full value is understated because the benefits of safer streets, better schools, stronger communities, and more active citizens are difficult to quantify and not seen immediately. The high return is part of the reason that more than 600 companies—from Microsoft to G.E. to local grocers—have supported local AmeriCorps programs. Stanley Litow, an officer of the IBM International Foundation, summed up his company's satisfaction by stating, "IBM expects a return on investment, and it bases its funding decisions on demonstrable results.... This program works."

Consider a program called L.A. Vets, which helps homeless Vietnam veterans become sober and independent. This nonprofit, established with the help of groups like the Disabled American Veterans, runs a 210-bed transitional home that provides 24-hour-a-day support, counseling, and job placement. Program managers conduct drug-testing regularly and expel those who flunk, a tough-love policy beyond the capacity of government bureaucracies. They require the veterans to maintain Westside Residence and pay $235 in rent, a demand that is both cost-effective and therapeutic. AmeriCorps didn't create this program but the 11 corps members at the Westside Residence, according to L.A. Vets' founders, have enabled them to start small businesses staffed by the veterans, stock a library, and make effective use of outside volunteers—including employees of a local computer business who teach the veterans how to repair computers. AmeriCorps members, in other words, have helped veterans become independent of government aid. As of this spring, only about one-quarter of the vets who moved in a year ago were back on the street. One-quarter were in treatment programs and half remained in transitional or independent housing, more sober and hopeful than they've been in years. And it's a good deal for taxpayers. The program has helped move more than 200 veterans out of veterans hospitals, where they would have cost the government $20,000 per year each.

About two-thirds of AmeriCorps projects address the problems of the young. AmeriCorps members tutor, operate after-school programs, work with gangs to reduce violence, create safe havens and safe corridors, and organize students to volunteer. Our record in these areas is one reason Governor Pete Wilson turned to the California Commission on Community Service to help reach his goal of providing at-risk youth in California with 250,000 mentors by the year 2000.

AmeriCorps changes those who perform the service. Full-time service, whether in AmeriCorps or in the armed forces, is a rite of passage that helps create well-rounded adults and citizens. They are expected to be resourceful and show leadership. On a more mundane level, they might learn practical skills—how to build a floor level, how to calm a crowd in an emergency, how to lead a team, or even how to show up on time.

For low-income youth, service provides a different experience than traditional government make-work jobs or training programs. AmeriCorps implicitly accepts conservative arguments against indiscriminate aid to the poor. All major religions teach that it is more blessed to give than receive. This is not only a moral instruction but a statement about human psychology: If you treat someone as a dependent, they will view themselves as such. Low-income citizens, who make up about a quarter of AmeriCorps volunteers, are earning a government benefit by serving, instead of being served. The principle was illustrated by a young high-school dropout, who left a street gang to join the Philadelphia Youth Service Corps. "Look, all my life people had been coming to help me," he said. "For the first time, this Corps asked me to do some good."

AmeriCorps teaches the right values. AmeriCorps challenges young people to give something to their community and country. It teaches them, in the words of William Buckley, to have "gratitude" for being given so much. It instills core values of hard work, discipline, and teamwork that make young people not only more productive workers but also better citizens.

AmeriCorps combats balkanization. By bringing people of different backgrounds together, AmeriCorps can combat ethnic and social fragmentation. Members who come to AmeriCorps from college quickly realize that the separatism they learned on

"AmeriCorps members tutor, operate after-school programs, work with gangs to reduce violence, create safe havens and safe corridors, and organize students to volunteer."

campus has to be replaced by teamwork. Here again, the goal is to replicate some of the successes of the military. The World War II draft was the nation's most effective class-mixing institution. The modern army is the most effective race-mixing institution. Because they are so focused on staying alive or achieving a military objective, soldiers inevitably have to focus on individual characteristics rather than group traits. National service can be the most effective means we have for dealing with our nation's racial problems. National service may ultimately replace affirmative action as the primary means for bridging the racial divide.

AmeriCorps expands educational opportunity. This is often cited as the main benefit of AmeriCorps, but it really doesn't make sense to spend $18,000 per member if the only benefit is extra college aid. However, the education award is proving to be an effective way of drawing people into service. And the AmeriCorps experience expands educational opportunity in a more subtle way—by raising the aspirations of those who serve. We have seen many individuals who decided to go to college because their service convinced them that they were capable of greater things. Many of them in turn impart this sense of broad horizons to elementary or high-school students they tutor.

Some conservatives have argued that even if AmeriCorps does worthwhile things now, it will inevitably evolve into a bloated bureaucracy that smothers local initiative. This is the strongest argument against AmeriCorps. Many an enterprise, public and private, that started out lean and flexible eventually became ossified.

AmeriCorps, though, will likely improve, not worsen, because of its basic structure. It is locally based and relies on a competitive grantmaking process. Two-thirds of the money goes directly to state commissions, which choose among competitive proposals from local nonprofit groups.

AmeriCorps is nonpartisan. By law, the state commissions comprise an equal number of Democrats and Republicans, appointed by governors—three-fifths of whom are currently Republicans. AmeriCorps supporters must acknowledge that the success of this program stems in no small part from the leadership of some Republican governors. And those who dislike this program must also recognize that "Bill Clinton's pet project," as it is so often called, is being shaped in large part by Republicans.

We at the Corporation have been willing to learn. The traditional government posture—cover up problems as quickly as possible—may work for a while, but it does not make for good programs. Among our mistakes:

We have taken too long to switch from an old-style government accounting system to a more rigorous, private-sector model. As a result, our books were recently found "unauditable" using the new accounting standards. We are now bringing in outside financial experts to make the Corporation a model of government financial accountability.

We funded a grant to Acorn Housing Corp., which is closely

associated with an advocacy agenda. When we found out that Acorn had crossed the line into political advocacy, we pulled the plug. (Among our 400 programs and 1,200 sites we have found only a handful that have engaged in political advocacy.)

We saw that some of our programs were spending too much money on management and overhead. So, we have told AmeriCorps's national and state grantees with above average costs that they must cut costs by 10 percent. And as part of our cost-cutting agreement with Senator Charles Grassley of Iowa, we've committed to specific average cost targets—$17,000 per member next year, $16,000 the next, and $15,000 in 1999.

In our first years, the programs raised $41 million from the private sector—$9 million more than the authorizing legislation required from all nonfederal sources—but some programs were relying too heavily on school districts, police departments, and other units of local government. So this year, we have required *all* of our programs to raise some money from the private sector.

Despite our efforts to make all our programs models of excellence, some did not succeed. So the Corporation for National Service or the state commissions stopped funding them. Fifty of the first-year AmeriCorps programs were not renewed—15 percent of the total. We realize that such a statistic can be used against us by our opponents. However, since the difference between business and government is the willingness to correct mistakes, this is probably the most businesslike thing we have done.

Having argued the substance of national service, I would like to close on a political note. House Republicans last year put themselves in an awkward position on AmeriCorps. They placed themselves on the wrong side of their own ideology, and played right into the old Democratic argument that Republicans are heartless and uninterested in solving social problems.

Republicans need not compound the error by giving this issue to Democrats. Voters do not automatically associate civilian service with Democrats. If Republicans embrace it, and put on their own imprint, people will look back 10 years from now and say AmeriCorps was a program that Democrats created and Republicans improved. Republicans could then be known as tough *and* compassionate, skeptical *and* wise. And along the way, Republicans will have truly helped transform the country from one that relies on government to solve problems to one that relies on citizen service.

"Fifty of the first-year AmeriCorps programs were not renewed— 15 percent of the total."

AmeriCorps the Beautiful?
National Service—or
Government Service?[6]

Service has a long and venerable history in the U.S., and it remains strong today. Three-quarters of American households give to charity. About 90 million adults volunteer; the value of their time has been estimated by the Independent Sector at nearly $200 billion.

Impressive as this is, it isn't enough to meet all of the pressing human needs that face our society. For example, Harris Wofford and Steven Waldman worry that the entry of women into the work force will reduce the number of volunteers. Hence, in their view, the need for a government program like the Corporation for National Service.

The desire to give Uncle Sam a senior management position in the service business goes back at least a century, to *Looking Backward*, a novel by lawyer and journalist Edward Bellamy. He envisioned compulsory service for all men and women between the ages of 21 and 45, resulting in a peaceful and prosperous utopia. *Looking Backward* was the best-selling book of its time and inspired the establishment of some 165 Bellamy clubs to push his egalitarian social system.

Two decades later, William James advocated the "moral equivalent of war," in which all young men would be required to work for the community. He argued that "the martial virtues, although originally gained by the race through war, are absolute and permanent human goods," and that national service could instill those same values in peacetime.

Most national service advocates today eschew such far-reaching utopian visions of social transformation. Nevertheless, the desire to create the good society through service lives on. Some advocates have seen national service as a means to provide training and employment, to encourage social equality, to promote civic-mindedness, or to expand access to college. Margaret Mead even saw it as a way to help liberate children from their parents. The legislative process always shrank such grandiose proposals into much more limited programs, such as the Peace Corps and, in 1993, the National and Community Service Trust Act, which established the Corporation for National and Community Service. But many of the grander goals remain—and are expressed by Wofford and Waldman: transforming participants, teaching values, combating balkanization, and expanding educa-

---

[6] Article by Doug Bandow, a senior fellow at the Cato Institute and the author of several books, including *The Politics of Envy: Statism as Theology*, from *Policy Review* 79:33-6 S/O '96. Copyright © 1996 *Policy Review*. Reprinted with permission.

tional opportunity.

Thus, the heritage of national service—this desire for government to promote ends other than service—is critical to understanding today's program and recognizing the pitfalls of government involvement. When we evaluate the Corporation and the thousands of AmeriCorps members, we must ask: service to whom and organized by whom?

Americans have worked in their communities since the nation's founding. Businesses, churches, and schools all actively help organize their members' efforts. Service in America is so vital because it is decentralized and privately organized, addresses perceived needs, and grows out of people's sense of duty and compassion. Any federal service program must be judged by whether it is consistent with this vision of volunteer service. Wofford and Waldman think yes. I'm less sanguine.

The mandatory variants of service obviously do not share this vision. In fact, the explicit goal of advocates of mandatory service programs was (and remains) to create a duty to the state rather than to the supposed beneficiaries of service. Moreover, service is to fit into a larger social plan implemented and enforced by government.

Of course, AmeriCorps is not mandatory, and Wofford and Waldman amass an impressive list of testimonials from private groups that welcome the Corporation's support. But, no one should be suprised that volunteer organizations might welcome financial assistance and "free" help. Washington's funds, however, could prove almost as powerful as its mandates in reshaping the independent sector. Some voluntary organizations recognize the danger. David King of the Ohio-West Virginia YMCA has warned: "The national service movement and the National Corporation are not about encouraging volunteering or community service. The national service movement is about institutionalizing federal funding for national and community service. It is about changing the language and understanding of service to eliminate the words 'volunteer' and 'community service' and in their place implant the idea that service is something paid for by the government."

King's fears are well founded. The history of the welfare state is the history of public enterprise pushing out private organization. The impact was largely unintentional, but natural and inevitable. Higher taxes left individuals with less money to give; government's assumption of responsibility for providing welfare shriveled the perceived duty of individuals to respond to their neighbors' needs; and the availability of public programs gave recipients an alternative to private assistance, one which did not challenge recipients to reform their destructive behavior.

The Corporation, despite the good intentions of people like Wofford and Waldman, risks doing the same thing to philanthropy. A federal "service" program risks teaching Americans that the duty of giving, and the job of deciding who is worthy to

"The national service movement is about institutionalizing federal funding for national and community service."

receive charity, belongs to government and not average people throughout society. At some point service to society could become widely equated with work for government.

Glimmerings of this problem have already surfaced. For instance, the Corporation treats "public" service as inherently better than private service. Service, however, comes in many forms. Being paid by the government to shelve books in a library, whether as an employee or as an AmeriCorps member, is no more laudable or valuable than being paid by Crown Books to stock bookshelves in a bookstore. A host of private-sector jobs provide enormous public benefits—consider health-care professionals, medical and scientific researchers, entrepreneurs, inventors, and artists. Many of these people earn less than they could in alternative work; they have chosen to serve in their own way. Yet government programs that equate public employment with service to society effectively denigrate service through private employment.

This public-sector bias is reflected in the fact that 2,800 of the first 20,000 AmeriCorps participants were assigned to federal agencies. For instance, the Department of the Interior used AmeriCorps workers to "update geological and hydrological information for the U.S. Geological Survey" and restore wetlands and wildlife habitat. Jobs like these are respectable, but they resemble traditional government employment rather than "service." While AmeriCorps participants may do good work as government employees, such activities are not likely to promote volunteerism around the country.

A more subtle problem is the likely long-term effect of federal funding on the volunteer groups and those who normally support volunteer groups. It is, in the abstract, hard to criticize grants to organizations like Habitat for Humanity (which until now refused to accept government funding), Big Brothers/Big Sisters, and the Red Cross. These groups do good work and money given to them is likely to be well spent.

Who, however, should do the giving? It is certainly simpler for the IRS to empty pockets nationwide and hand a bit of the tax haul to the Corporation, which, in turn, gives it to charity. But the right way is for individuals to send their money directly to deserving groups. That Habitat for Humanity could use more full-time employees to supervise its ample private volunteers is understandable; that it should turn to the government for the resources to hire those volunteers is not.

Indeed, at its most basic level, real charity doesn't mean giving away someone else's money. As Marvin Olasky has pointed out, compassion once meant to "suffer with." Over time it came to mean writing a check. Now it seems to be equated with making someone else write a check. At least public welfare programs are theoretically accountable to taxpayers for their activities. But collecting taxes for private charities, especially those with philosophical or theological viewpoints that may conflict with those

"While AmeriCorps participants may do good work as government employees, such activities are not likely to promote volunteerism around the country."

of many taxpayers, is especially dubious.

Nor is dependence on government healthy for private philanthropic groups. Although they get to choose and train volunteers funded by the Corporation, it seems inevitable that government will end up favoring some activities and disfavoring others. Such preferences may not be nefarious, but groups will be tempted to adjust their mission to become eligible for federal funding.

Even if the Corporation eschews the natural temptation to meddle, the behavior of recipients is likely to change. Groups will be tempted to shift their fundraising from private appeals to "public education" and formal lobbying. After all, government checks tend to be much larger and cheaper to obtain than private donations.

Wofford and Waldman contend that government funding will prevent private groups from becoming bureaucratic by furnishing them with short-term volunteers, who won't develop "a careerist mindset." It's not clear why career volunteers would be a problem. In fact, some problems are better met by experienced volunteers. Surely volunteer groups, if they found careerism to be a problem, could, if adequately funded, hire precisely the sort of people who now join AmeriCorps. Money does not have to be funneled through government to ensure that private groups receive "new energy," as Wofford and Waldman put it.

Moreover, government's growing role in funding private groups, however worthy, is likely to encourage people to further abdicate their civic responsibilities. If we are serious about strengthening civil society and reviving a sense of individual duty to help those in need, we must emphasize contributing as well as volunteering. People will feel less pressure to volunteer time and money if the government not only provides public welfare programs but funds charitable groups. Wofford and Waldman cite private support for local AmeriCorps programs as evidence of their value. But AmeriCorps isn't necessary for IBM, G.E., Microsoft, and local grocers to support service programs. Private-sector funding should preempt, not follow, government involvement.

Boosting contributions will address one of the problems that Wofford and Waldman mention: the increase in women who have entered the work force and therefore have less time to volunteer. If they are working, they should have more money to contribute, and they should be encouraged to do so, thereby helping to fund full-time volunteers.

In fact, thoughtfully choosing which charities to support, and monitoring their activities are themselves important forms of volunteerism. Sending money off to Washington for distribution to private groups benefits the recipients, but no one else. By contrast, the sinews of community grow stronger when people stay informed, give voluntarily, and get involved. As we attempt to shrink the welfare state, getting more people to give more and to take more time considering where to give should be one of our highest priorities.

Finally, AmeriCorps may have undesirable consequences on volunteers. Undoubtedly, many volunteers paid by the government really believe in what they are doing. But the Corporation has turned service into a job, one that, counting the tax-free voucher, pays more than other entry-level employment. Some participants have privately admitted that they see national service as a remunerative job option, not a unique opportunity to help the community. Indeed, much of the president's pitch during the campaign was framed in terms of naked self-interest: earning credit toward college tuition. There's nothing wrong with joining AmeriCorps to do so, of course. But doing so really isn't more noble than, say, pumping gas for the same reason.

"There is no guarantee that taxpayer-funded 'service' will be worth its cost."

Indeed, government-funded service plays into what some national-service proponents have denounced as an entitlement mentality—the idea that, for instance, students have a right to a taxpayer-paid education. Some advocates of national service have rightly asked: Why should middle-class young people be able to force poor taxpayers to help put them through school? But public "service" jobs sweetened with a salary and an educational grant are no solution: they merely transform the kind of employment that a young person seeks to help cover his educational expenses. Some AmeriCorps volunteers do sacrifice, but there is no real sacrifice involved in, say, informing people about the availability of Federal Emergency Management Agency service centers, maintaining vehicles, surveying residents about recreational interests, cutting vegetation, and changing light bulbs in dilapidated schools—all activities funded by the Corporation. In contrast, consider the sort of tasks envisioned by William James: young laborers would be sent off "to coal and iron mines, to freight trains, to fishing fleets in December."

The real solution to the entitlement mentality is not to say that students are entitled to taxpayer aid as long as they work for the government for a year or two, but to rethink who deserves the subsidy. We also need to explore how federal educational assistance may have actually made it harder for students to afford college by fueling tuition hikes (the schools, of course, are the ultimate beneficiaries of most student aid). And we have to address the host of other "entitlements" that riddle the federal budget and sap people's independence.

Finally, there is the more practical question as to whether taxpayers are likely to get their money's worth from the service provided by AmeriCorps members. Wofford and Waldman cite impressive statistics about trees planted and beaches restored, and there's no doubt that much good work has and will be done by AmeriCorps volunteers. But there is no guarantee that taxpayer-funded "service" will be worth its cost.

Consider the opportunity costs of national service. "Public service" has a nice ring to it, but a dollar going to national service will not necessarily yield more benefits than an additional dollar spent on medical research, technological innovation, business investment, or any number of other private and public purposes. Nor is hiring, say, a potential doctor to spend a year surveying residents, handling paperwork, or replacing light bulbs necessarily a good deal—in terms of economics or service.

Unfortunately, some waste is almost inevitable. Local organizations are not likely to use essentially "free" labor from the federal government as efficiently as if they had to cover the costs themselves, because staff members will be tempted to assign work they prefer not to do themselves to the subsidized outsiders. For example, in Orange County, California, the Civic Center Barrio Housing Corp. used AmeriCorps personnel to solicit donations and handle paperwork. Corporation critics have, in fact, generated their own roll of waste to counter Wofford and Waldman's list of successes.

Another potentially important opportunity cost is the diversion of bright men and women from the military. The end of the Cold War has sharply cut recruiting requirements, but it has also reduced the perceived national need. As a result, the armed forces have had greater difficulty in attracting quality recruits. Yet various programs of educational benefits have always been an important vehicle for drawing college-capable youth into the military. Providing similar benefits for civilian service is likely to hinder recruiting for what remains the most fundamental form of national service—defending the nation. Surveys have found that a majority of potential recruits would consider joining AmeriCorps rather than the armed forces because they see it as a better way to gain educational assistance.

If AmeriCorps is not the answer, what is? First, government barriers in the way of private individuals and groups who want to help should be torn down. Minimum-wage laws effectively forbid the hiring of dedicated but unskilled people; every increase makes this problem worse. Restrictions on paratransit operations limit private transportation for the disabled. Regulations also hinder other forms of volunteerism. Unnecessary health department restrictions prevent restaurants in Los Angeles and elsewhere from donating food to the hungry, for instance. In short, in many cases important needs are unmet precisely because of perverse government policy.

Second, leaders throughout society, from lawmakers to clerics to philanthropists to corporate presidents, need to emphasize that the ultimate responsibility to help those in need lies with individuals, families, and communities, not government. They need to create a more traditional sense of compassion, the idea that charity requires personal commitment—both in volunteering time and exercising careful stewardship over charitable contributions. This requires highlighting the needs of the disadvantaged and groups seeking to help the disadvantaged, and emphasizing that people can no longer act as if they "gave at the office" through government.

"Various programs of educational benefits have always been an important vehicle for drawing college-capable youth into the military."

Third, policymakers need to consider tax incentives, particularly tax credits for charitable donations, to encourage people to volunteer their money. A goal of $500 million in new contributions—a mere $2 a person and more than now spent by the Corporation—might be a reasonable start.

Finally, to the extent that serious social problems remain, government should use narrowly targeted responses to meet the most serious problems. That is, it would be better to find a way to attract several thousand people to help care for the terminally ill than to lump that task in with teaching, planting trees, changing light bulbs, administrative work, and scores of other jobs to be solved by a force of tens or hundreds of thousands.

AmeriCorps was created with the best of intentions. But the Corporation for National Service cannot escape its statist heritage: it promotes service, but shifts the center of gravity in the volunteer community from civil to political society. What we need instead is a renewed commitment to individual service. People, in community with one another, need to help meet the many serious social problems that beset us. But private activism needs neither oversight nor subsidy from Uncle Sam. Some of the volunteerism can be part-time and some full-time; some can take place within the family, some within churches, and some within civic and community groups. Some may occur through profit-making ventures.

The point is, there is no predetermined definition of service, pattern of appropriate involvement, set of "needs" to be met or tasks to be fulfilled. America's strength is its combination of humanitarian impulses, private association, and diversity. We need service, not "national service."

III. Volunteerism Is Not Enough

Editor's Introduction

Volunteerism does a tremendous amount of good for the United States; however, it cannot be counted on to solve all of America's problems completely. There will have to be more than just feel-good sentiment to promote volunteerism. Youth mentoring, which could be one of the most effective and useful of services, needs more than well-intentioned volunteers, for example. Mentoring is not an activity for occasional spare-time hours; in order to have a positive effect, mentors need supporting structures. The articles of Section III show that any serious campaign to save America's children would still need the support of Washington's money along with millions of volunteers.

To begin with, volunteerism appears to be inefficient when viewed in market terms. Ineffective management of time and money have made it difficult to solve some of the most critical problems known today. Section III's first article, by Michael J. Gerson from *U.S. News & World Report*, reports that volunteers can work wonders, yet they are not always ready for what is demanded of them—bridging the gaps left behind by welfare and other government programs. Volunteers are also not expected to care for at-risk children and abandoned seniors, who require "one-on-one attention for long periods of time." Gerson believes that in order for volunteering to make any progress, volunteers must be motivated to work beyond the call of duty and if not for their own sakes, for the benefit of others. The article also gives one volunteer's personal account of volunteering along with a brief guide on becoming a successful volunteer.

The government would teach children to read under President Clinton's recently proposed "America Reads Challenge," and AmeriCorps workers would supervise the volunteers they recruit, mostly college students. An article by Robert W. Sweet, Jr., from *Policy Review*, criticizes Clinton's proposed solution to the 40 percent of third-grade students that cannot read: volunteers. Although the president's intent is noble, Sweet believes the responsibility of the public education system should be a more concentrated effort and its "single most important mission."

"The practice of selfless giving actually pre-dates the Clinton years," Matthew Scully states facetiously in an article from *National Review*, which evaluates the Presidents' Summit for America's Future held in 1997 in Philadelphia. President Clinton believes that it is *not enough* for corporate America to donate money to good causes and leave it at that. Instead, there must be a global strategy, a broad network, more conferences, and more speeches until cynicism has been defeated once and for all. Scully criticizes the Clintons for taking too much credit for the volunteer summit. "They never merely adopt causes, the Clintons, they absorb them until everything is soaked in sentimentality and self-regard," Scully writes.

According to reports, millions of U.S. children live in poverty and the numbers have increased measurably in just the past few years. In an article from *Christianity Today*, Richard A. Kauffman analyzes these pressing needs. Kauffman charges that the faith community and corporate America were given little opportunity to become involved in the follow-up to the Presidents' Summit for America's Future, which hopes to recruit two million volunteers by the year 2000. Society as a whole, including public and private sectors, together with the church, the author concludes, must work together to create equal opportunity for all.

Colin Powell and his nonprofit group, America's Promise, have set out to help two million children by the year 2000. Mark Stricherz from the *New Republic* examines Powell's new program, which is funded entirely through volunteerism and private charity. According to Stricherz, the campaign has been making progress, but corporations have given practically nothing. A major difficulty, the author believes, is that corporate leaders prefer to support their own favorite causes, which tend to be more concerned with image than with the needs of impoverished children. America's Promise attempts to ensure that corporations are actually directing their efforts toward needy children, but as the organization's officials have conceded, it has no systematic way to verify their pledges. Powell has the potential to make an impact by using American volunteers as his social force, but the author wonders if the private sector can realistically be relied upon to document its efforts.

Other countries have also cut social spending. The Canadian government, for example, planned in 1996 to cut approximately one-third of the $17 billion it gives annually to the provinces over the next two years. The final article of Section III, by Anthony Wilson-Smith from *Maclean's*, assesses how these cuts will affect nearly all Canadians in some way. Provinces will cut services and subsidies, and the many volunteer groups that depend on money from these levels of government could be devastated.

Do Do-Gooders Do Much Good?[1]

Most Volunteers Aren't Solving
Care Problems

If you think volunteerism is noncontroversial, listen to Pastor Eugene F. Rivers III of the Azusa Christian Community in Boston. He has undertaken what he calls a jihad to reclaim troubled kids from gangs and drugs. It has earned him bullets through his front window and a reputation for bluntness. It has not earned him much help from middle-class suburbanites. Such people, he says, are more interested in "recreational volunteerism," devoting their time and money to "MOMA (Museum of Modern Art), Mass General Hospital, or Lincoln Center, and saving whales with one fin."

When his anger subsides, Rivers asks a potent question: "If there are really 93 million volunteers in America then why are our cities worse than they have ever been?"

There is hardly a member of Congress who hasn't used that 93 million number, which was generated by Independent Sector, a group that studies and represents nonprofit organizations. The survey estimated that those Americans contributed a stunning 20.3 billion hours of their time in 1995—218 hours per person. A closer look shows why Rivers's question is so penetrating. First, about 4.6 billion of those hours are informal volunteering, things like baby-sitting for a neighbor and baking cookies for a school fair. The 20 billion number also includes volunteers at theaters, museums, and other cultural institutions, plus serving on boards and commissions. Indeed, only 8.4 percent of those 93 million volunteers work in "human services," a broad category that includes aiding the homeless, family counseling, and helping the Red Cross. Fewer than 4 percent of volunteers work as tutors and just 1.2 percent as mentors or substance-abuse-prevention counselors—about half as many as help in theaters, music, and the arts. A separate estimate of volunteering through churches found the same pattern. Lester Salamon, director of the Institute for Policy Studies at Johns Hopkins University, says that roughly 7 percent to 15 percent of volunteering done through churches goes outside the walls of the sanctuary into the community. Most volunteers help the men's club and choir, not the downtown soup kitchen.

One on one. For years, conservatives have argued that volunteers should shoulder more of the social welfare burden, and government less. This notion has never been more widely

[1] Article by Michael J. Gerson, policy director for Senator Dan Coats (R) Indiana, with Paul Glastris, Josh Chetwynd, Susannah Fox, Eric Ransdell, and Warren Cohen; from *U.S. News & World Report* 122:26-30+ Ap 28 '97. Copyright © 1997 *U.S. News & World Report*. Reprinted with permission.

accepted, as evidenced by the strong bipartisan support for the President's Summit for America's Future—also known as the volunteer summit. In a show of unity usually reserved for state funerals, every living ex-president, with the exception of Ronald Reagan, who will be represented by his wife, will stand with President Clinton in Independence Hall in Philadelphia this Monday to salute mentors, tutors, and other involved citizens.

There are many acknowledged benefits of volunteering. It helps build a sense of community, breaks down barriers between people, and often raises the quality of life. Some types of volunteer activities seem consistently successful, the most obvious example being the outpouring of help that surrounds natural disasters like the floods currently hitting the upper Midwest. But policy makers are now relying on volunteers to do far more. "If all 200 million Americans gave three hours a month," Newt Gingrich has said, "there would be 600 million voluntary hours a month to find a child and teach it to read, a drug addict to get off drugs, or a poor person to teach how to be profitable." President Clinton has set similarly high expectations. "If every church in America hired just one family, the welfare problem would go way down."

It is one thing to celebrate volunteers. It is another thing to depend upon them to fill the gaps left by failures and cutbacks in welfare and other government programs. In this light, it is decidedly not the thought that counts. Volunteerism is often understood as a virtue, but now it should also be understood as a market. And viewed that way, it is an inefficient one. Most volunteers are not deployed effectively to solve the hardest, and most critical, problems. Management is often poor, and amazingly little is known about which volunteer programs really work. To an extent rarely acknowledged publicly, especially by many conservatives, the volunteer sector is not ready for the responsibilities now being thrust upon it.

Sometimes volunteers are in abundance. When disasters strike, there is never any shortage of volunteers to fill sandbags and comfort victims. Habitat for Humanity rarely has trouble attracting volunteers on weekends. One-time events like AIDS walkathons and "Net Days" to wire schools for computers can make an enormous difference in a short amount of time, and they usually draw a big crowd.

But the problems of troubled children, needy seniors, and the poor require a different type of volunteering: It must be performed one on one, over a long period of time, and, often, in low-income neighborhoods. And for this type of assistance, there is a shortage of volunteers. A telling case is that of Big Brothers/Big Sisters, a demonstrably successful volunteer effort. Among children who spent 18 months in the Big Brothers/Big Sisters program, initial drug use was cut 46 percent and initial alcohol use cut by 27 percent, according to a major 1995 study by Public/Private Ventures. Participating children skipped half as

"Volunteerism is often understood as a virtue, but now it should also be understood as a market."

many days of school and were a third less likely to hit someone. All this in an organization with a universally recognized brand name and a notable absence of scandal. Yet Big Brothers currently has 30,000 children waiting to be matched with adults. And the group estimates that as many as 15 million children could benefit from having mentors.

Why are supply and demand so misaligned? The simplest explanation is that volunteers sign up for reasons other than the urgency of social problems. Volunteers say they participate because a) they were asked by someone; b) they learned of an opportunity through an organization to which they belonged; or c) a family member or friend would benefit as a result. And these reasons tend to limit volunteering to a tight circle of familiar friends, places, and institutions. "There is very little commuting to do volunteer work," says Julian Wolpert, a professor at Princeton University who has written extensively on the non-profit sector. While the Good Samaritan only had to cross the street, many volunteers must cross to the other side of the tracks.

Volunteers sometimes fear that if they visit neighborhoods with high crime rates they may suffer violence, or at least antagonism. Robert Todd, a white businessman who tutors at a largely Hispanic school in Dallas, tells of arriving on the day that a major fire consumed a car dealership down the street. Finding the children excited, he asked one of them why and was told, "Because the white man's business is burning down."

"Horror stories." Economic realities shape the choices volunteers can make. The backbone of volunteer involvement in the past was stay-at-home mothers with flexible schedules. Now, with both parents working, whatever spare time is left over must go to the kids. "I don't think it is a question of people not wanting to volunteer; it is a question of how, where, and can I do it in a way that fits into my schedule," says Kathy Behrens, vice chairwoman of City Cares of America, a group that hooks up busy people with appropriate volunteer opportunities. City Cares now has chapters in a number of cities, including Atlanta, Washington, and Philadelphia, and puts 75,000 volunteers to work. Behrens estimates that about half those people do just a single day of work during the year.

Such once-a-year volunteers can be usefully deployed at routine tasks, like dishing out food in a soup kitchen or removing graffiti, but do not help with more complicated human interventions. And that's a significant loss. Research has shown that mentoring and tutoring depend for their success on the duration and consistency of personal involvement. In tutoring, for example, the six or eight hours of school each day is already a huge part of a child's life. "If it is already failing to teach at that level of intensity, it won't be helped by another 15 minutes with a tutor," says Lance Potter, director of evaluation at the Corporation for National Service. Potter estimates that the lowest level of tutoring that is still effective is somewhere between 30 and 60 minutes per session, at least two or three times a week. "Much below that," he says, "you are not really helping, and you may be hurting." That's because ineffective tutoring can actually harm self-esteem. Children who have inconsistent or unreliable tutors will view it as further evidence of the unreliability of adults. But few tutoring programs consistently attract volunteers for long periods of time.

While we know the general characteristics of what makes successful volunteering, we know little about what programs pull it off. "Most of the information is anecdotal," says William Niederloh, chief executive officer of the National Results Council, a new research group that studies social programs. Barbara Wasik of Johns Hopkins University recently analyzed every known study of tutoring programs and concluded that only two could, using rigorous evaluation techniques, prove efficacy. One of them was the Good News After School Reading Program in Chicago. Volunteers come two days a week, for an hour and a half each day, often from affluent suburbs nearby. They are carefully trained and use materials prepared by professional staff, one of whom is always there during the tutoring sessions. "Our tutors aren't floundering around," says Betty Boyd, a cosupervisor of the program.

> *"People in high-crime areas were reluctant to organize, often distrusting their neighbors and refusing to attend or host community meetings."*

A few other studies raise questions about volunteer effectiveness. One recent analysis found that Neighborhood Watch programs, in which residents help patrol a community, have little measurable effect on crime. People in high-crime areas were reluctant to organize, often distrusting their neighbors and refusing to attend or host community meetings. Wealthier areas, in which trust was higher, generally had little crime to begin with. And one 1990 study of Neighborhood Watch argued that the program, in some cases, increased the fear of crime rather than relieving it.

In a commercial marketplace, consumers help ensure quality by rewarding the good and punishing the bad. But people who would never buy a CD player without reading *Consumer Reports* join volunteer efforts without a way of knowing what impact they'll have. Indeed, the very quality that makes volunteering so noble—the selflessness—undermines the efficiency of the market. "It is not outcomes that matter to me," says Sara Mann, a student at Southern Methodist University who regularly volunteers. "It's more personal than that. It's the encouragement you get out of it."

And perhaps it is unrealistic to expect each volunteer to conduct personalized cost-benefit analyses. Volunteers don't think in those terms, nor should they. Some actions are taken out of simple decency. "I know the (children) face hardships," says Lee Pease, who volunteers at the Alpha Child Care Center for children in crisis run by Mission Arlington, a Christian social-service group in Arlington, Texas. "But I don't have the power to change that, other than the one moment I am holding that child. I am in charge of that one moment. And it keeps you coming back."

For more occasional volunteers, however, ineffectiveness can be a real disincentive to come back. According to a new *U.S. News* poll, 20 percent of those who had volunteered in the past year said they had cut back because they weren't sure if their work was helping solve a problem.

If volunteers can't always assess outcomes, who should? Charities themselves don't do rigorous self-analysis for understandable reasons. Sometimes effectiveness is inherently difficult to measure. What is the measurable outcome of working in a hospice? Many nonprofits are cash-strapped and struggling to perform basic services and can't afford to spend time or money on evaluation. Others avoid assessment simply because they can. "People can get away with all sorts of things sending out pictures of starving kids," says Charles W. Colson, chairman of Prison Fellowship Ministries.

In a significant shift, United Way has begun a massive effort to get its member charities to measure outcomes. In the past, to the extent anything was measured it was the "input" (how many hours did the tutor work?) not the "outcome" (did he or she raise the reading scores of the child?). So far, however, only 200 of the 1,200 United Way programs are fully participating.

Foundations, which would seem to have an interest in tracking the soundness of their investments, have done little study because they focus more on stimulating innovative ideas than on assessing old ones. "The normal practice," says Princeton Prof. John DiIulio, "has been to give money to people you've never met, in places you've never been, with results you've never tried to measure."

The efficiency of a market also depends on effective management, and the lack of good volunteer management is one of the consistent topics of self-criticism in the nonprofit world. One Independent Sector survey found that in 1,300 nonprofits, fewer than half of their chief executives could say how many volunteers worked at their organizations or how many hours' worth of time they donated.

This neglect often limits the contributions of volunteers and the quality of their experiences. "I got on board with a local home care organization and had no guidance or training," says Nan Hawthorne, a volunteer in Seattle. "I found myself in a very emotional situation without any tools or guidance. I went over to this man's house five days a week. No one told me that one day a week is the norm. I burned out quickly and left the group." Hawthorne heard so many other "horror stories" about people's volunteer experiences that she formed Sound Volunteer Management to train volunteer coordinators.

When Lisa Rapaszky, 24, volunteered at an Oakland, Calif., emergency shelter for women and children, she discovered that her overworked supervisor had no time to train her. Yet after three weeks, Rapaszky was virtually running the place. From 8 a.m. to 4 p.m. each day, she was left almost alone in the shelter to do everything from answering the phones to helping drug addicts. "You had the least-qualified person during the most intense part of the day," she says. "These were women twice my age, twice my size, some of them just out of jail, and I'm telling them what to do."

Insatiable appetite. But good training can be expensive. In Big Brother/Big Sisters, the process of screening, training, matching, and supervising volunteers costs about $1,000 per match. If Big Brothers were to get all the volunteers it could handle to cover the 30,000 children waiting for matches, the bill would be $30 million.

In other cases, nonprofit managers really don't want to give volunteers meaningful work. Jeanne Bradner, a nonprofit consultant in Chicago, concludes that many organizations have "staff infection," which she defines as an insatiable appetite for more paid staff. "Their attitude toward volunteers is often that anything which is free can't be valuable." In one survey, 80 percent of nonprofit managers said they didn't believe volunteers could be substituted extensively for paid professionals in nonprofit organizations without a significant decline in quality.

"The impulse to emphasize credentialed professionals over volunteers can undermine innovative community efforts."

The impulse to emphasize credentialed professionals over volunteers can undermine innovative community efforts. In Texas in 1995, Teen Challenge, a religiously oriented drug treatment program with strong outcomes since 1969, was informed by the Commission on Alcohol and Drug Abuse that it would need to hire credentialed counselors or face fines and imprisonment. (The decision was later overturned by Gov. George W. Bush.)

These nagging management concerns gain an added degree of urgency in light of the summit. "The real question," says Rebecca Rimel of the Pew Charitable Trusts, which is helping to finance the summit, "is if the nonprofit community is prepared for the influx of volunteers." Summit organizers are emphasizing not vague volunteerism but increased adult involvement in children's lives. This is a good sign. Says Princeton's DiIulio: "When you boil down the last 50 years of empirical research on what works to improve the lives of children, there is one conclusion: No program, public or private, that fails to build meaningful relationships between responsible adults and young people works."

Can this type of hands-on volunteer involvement be expanded to cope with the enormous need? That is the vital question, says Gary Walker of Public/Private Ventures: "Whenever you have time-limited disasters, volunteers turn out to be amazingly efficient. When you convert that into social problems—not two days on a levee but six months with a youth—can you go to a big enough scale? I just don't know."

Volunteerism can be unfocused or powerful, oversold or indispensable, "recreational" or transformational. There is a wide gap between the emotional investment required for a day of cleaning a park and years of working with another human being. Yet the latter is the form of volunteering most likely to get at society's core problems. These approaches have not been tried and found wanting; they have been tried and found difficult. Perhaps the greatest challenge facing the Philadelphia summit—and the volunteer sector as a whole—is whether Americans can be motivated not just to volunteer but to sacrifice.

ONE VOLUNTEER:
"Dear Diary, I Detest Being Near Them."

Jennifer Brophy, now a 19-year-old sophomore at Ball State University in Muncie, Ind., kept a diary while serving as a volunteer tutor for a ninth-grade "directed" (remedial) science class at Middletown High School near Frederick, Md. The names of the children have been changed. This excerpt is from a forthcoming anthology on volunteer service compiled by Suzanne Goldsmith, the editor of Dig, *a Des Moines-based newsletter about community building.*

Feb. 21, 1994: Today was my first day of tutoring and what a day it was! I like Mrs. Oakes a lot. She is sweet and understanding and seems to love what she does. The students are a different story. They obviously resent Laurie's and my presence. They probably feel they don't need our help and by our being there, they are in some way stupid. We are definitely very unwelcome.

Feb. 24, 1994: I finally feel somewhat useful. The class did a lab on friction, and I was able to help Josh with his calculations. He was impressed by my calculator.

March 4, 1994: Overall, tutoring is not what I expected. I thought the students would look up to me because I was older and could help them get through this course with a passing grade. This could not have been further from the truth. They are disrespectful, loud, annoying, and I detest being near them.... The students push us away. I'm almost scared to help because the kids are so rude.... If I were the teacher of this class, a large majority of the students would be in the office with referrals. I can't help feeling so frustrated...I will not give up!!

March 23, 1994: The only thing that gets me through the period is the response I get from Alan and David. They now listen to me, show occasional respect, and converse with me regarding outside activities. They have accepted me and because of this acceptance, I can at times effectively tutor them.

April 19, 1994: Today's class was very disturbing because I saw three students purposely fail their tests. Linda, Ashley and Ann filled in any answer in order to finish quickly.

April 26, 1994: I'm ecstatic! I can't get over how well Alan is responding to me. I look back and remember thinking he was hopeless. He is nice to me and shows me respect in his own way. I almost enjoy tutoring now. I feel that I'm starting to make a difference.

June 6, 1994: David decided to cooperate with me, and we got further than anybody else. He's bossy—and I shouldn't put up with him telling me what to do. But he probably needs somebody to listen to him. I'm certain he will do well on the final if he applies himself, and decides to care. I would like to learn more about motivating students to want to succeed and to stay in school. I want to be able to serve the students next year so much better!

How to Be a Successful Volunteer: A Guide

The road to volunteer hell is paved with good intentions. Ask any kind soul who has shown up for a stint to save the world and instead found chaos—no training, no agenda, no thanks for coming. Here are five guidelines toward an effective volunteer experience, gleaned from academics who study volunteerism, volunteer coordinators, and vexed volunteers.

• **Shop around.** Experts endorse the weed-whacker method for finding a well-run volunteer agency: Just as you'd chat with friends about their weed whackers before buying one, talk to acquaintances about their volunteer experiences. The local United Way, the mayor's office, or a neighborhood school also might point to outstanding agencies. Or try Web sites with volunteer opportunities, like

SERVEnet
(*http://www.servenet.org/*)

and IdeaLIST
(*http://www.contact.org/*);

U.S. News Online
(*http://www.usnews.com*)

has links to other such sites. Once you've picked a group, ask a volunteer: "What bugs you—and what gives you pleasure—in your work?"

• **Know thy skills and schedule.** Obvious, essential, and often overlooked advice. Do you have abilities you'd like to use in a volunteer setting? Do you hate fund-raising? Are you better suited to a one-shot gig, like a walkathon for the hungry? Or are you seeking an intense challenge, like teaching a child to read—and if so, do you really have the time? (Veteran volunteers advise starting small and working up to a more time consuming commitment.) At the same time, don't be guided only by what you want to do, counsels Paul Schervish, director of Boston College's Social Welfare Research Institute. "The question is what is needed by those you serve."

• **Be prepared.** Or as the Sufis say, "Trust in God but tie up your camel." A first-rate agency will provide training to help you succeed as a volunteer, from a 15-minute lecture on soup-kitchen etiquette to a series of seminars for a prospective mentor. The volunteer, meanwhile, should pursue the practical side of service. What is the job description? And how should you handle difficult situations—say, if a child you are tutoring asks for money?

• **Expect respect.** "I believe in altruism, but it fades quickly," says Ram Cnaan, an associate professor at the University of Pennsylvania School of Social Work. Volunteers won't stick around if staffers talk down to them ("Oh, they're just the volunteers") or fail to thank them. The beleaguered volunteer should complain to someone in authority, he says. If the gripe is ignored, "then you walk."

• **Be sure you make a difference.** Ask the group for its mission statement, then ask how the volunteer work fulfills the mission, says Nan Hawthorne, managing director of Sound Volunteer Management in Seattle. If volunteers are truly to make a difference, the agency should regularly meet with them—and listen when they have something to say.

—Marc Silver

Don't Read, Don't Tell: Clinton's Phony War on Illiteracy[2]

"Under [Clinton's] proposed 'America Reads Challenge,' the government would recruit a million volunteers...to teach children to read under the direction of AmeriCorps workers.

President Clinton is to be congratulated for calling attention to a national disaster: the inability of 40 percent of American eight-year-olds to read on their own. Reading is the gateway skill. It opens the door to all other learning. It is essential for participation in the knowledge-based economy of the next century. The president is right to insist that every American child learn this indispensable skill by the end of the third grade.

But the president's answer for this disaster does not provide a real solution. Under his proposed "America Reads Challenge," the government would recruit a million volunteers, many of them minimally trained college students, to teach children to read under the direction of AmeriCorps workers. The program sounds wonderful—we're all for voluntarism. But it diverts accountability from the colossal failure of the public-education system to achieve perhaps its single most important mission.

Think about it. Forty percent of third-graders cannot read. What a terrible indictment of our public-education system! What more important responsibility do schools have than to teach reading? Almost every child can learn to read by the end of first grade, if properly taught. But schools aren't achieving this by the third grade. For this failure, heads should roll. All teachers or principals or school superintendents who have failed to teach 40 percent of their third-graders to read should be looking for a new job. If 40 percent of third-graders cannot read and nothing has been done about it already, then teachers and principals obviously aren't being held to the right standards of performance.

Even more important, current methods for teaching reading must be completely overhauled. There are now 825,000 teachers from kindergarten to third grade whose principal job is to teach the three Rs. A high percentage of these teachers have master's degrees; almost all have been specially trained to teach reading. Obviously their training isn't working.

The federal government already spends $8.3 billion on 14 programs that concentrate on promoting literacy, including Title I funding for school districts with high proportions of low-income or poorly performing students. If 40 percent of third-graders can't read, then this money has not been wisely targeted and the teaching philosophy must be faulty.

Federal, state, and local governments spend another $40 billion a year on special education, with about half targeted at children with "specific learning disabilities." According to J.W. Lerner,

[2] Article by Robert W. Sweet, Jr., president of the National Right to Read Foundation, former director of the National Institute of Education under President Reagan, and federal Administrator for Juvenile Justice Programs under President Bush; from *Policy Review* 83:38-42 My/Je '97. Copyright © 1997 *Policy Review*. Reprinted with permission.

writing in the *Journal of the American Academy of Child and Adolescent Psychiatry*, "80 percent of children identified as having learning disabilities have their primary difficulties in learning to read." Special-education reading methods don't seem to be working very well, either. According to research by B.A. Shaywitz and S.E. Shaywitz, more than 40 percent of high-school students identified as "learning disabled" drop out of school prior to graduation; only 17 percent enroll in any postsecondary course, 6 percent participate in two-year higher-education programs, and 1.8 percent in four-year programs. The loss of human potential is staggering.

The 1993 National Assessment of Education Progress reported that "70 percent of fourth-graders, 30 percent of eighth-graders, and 64 percent of 12th-graders did not...attain a proficient level of reading." These students have not attained the minimum level of skill in reading considered necessary to do the academic work at their grade level. The National Adult Literacy Survey (NALS), released in 1993, revealed that between 40 million and 44 million Americans are unable to read phone books, ballots, car manuals, nursery rhymes, the Declaration of Independence, the Bible, the Constitution, or the directions on a medicine bottle. Another 50 million Americans recognize so few printed words that they are limited to a fourth- or fifth-grade level of reading. Illiterates account for 75 percent of unemployed adults, 33 percent of mothers receiving Aid to Families with Dependent Children, 85 percent of juveniles who appear in court, and 60 percent of prison inmates.

How has a nation that has dedicated so many resources to education allowed illiteracy to grow to such an unprecedented level? We can solve illiteracy now. Poor people, rich people, rural residents and city dwellers, all have an equal opportunity to master the skill of reading, if they are properly taught.

A Simple Solution

There's no great mystery to teaching reading. It's as easy as a, b, c. The best approach for the overwhelming majority of children is systematic phonics, the simple concept of teaching the 26 letters of the alphabet, the 44 sounds they make, and the 70 most common ways to spell those sounds. For most children, learning this basic code unlocks 85 percent of the words in the English language by the end of the first grade. Although some words such as "sugar" or "friend" have irregular spellings, children of all levels of intelligence can learn to read most words simply by learning the correspondence between sounds and letters.

This is the great benefit of an alphabet. Historian David Diringer has called the alphabet "the most important invention in the social history of the world." Ancient Egyptians had to memorize hundreds of hieroglyphics. Chinese and Japanese citizens must learn thousands of characters and character-combinations to function in society. It can be done, but with enormous difficulty. Reading in English is simple and accessible to almost everybody if properly taught.

An emphasis on phonics once made America the most literate nation on earth. From colonial times until the latter part of the 19th century, reading instruction was simple and straightforward: Teach the code, then have children read. It worked then; it will work now. Immigrants from every nation on earth had come to America. They all wanted to learn English, and most of them did. Millions of Americans used Noah Webster's *Blue Backed Speller*, a simple systematic phonics book, to teach their children to read at home or at school. More than 24 million copies were sold. It was second in sales only to the Bible.

"The premise...was that children could learn to read by associating words with pictures."

With phonics the predominant instructional practice, illiteracy was almost unknown at the turn of the century among those who attended school. In 1910, the U.S. Bureau of Education reported, only 2.2 percent of schoolchildren between the ages of 10 and 14 in the U.S. were illiterate. Blacks had been forbidden to read under slavery, and only 4 percent of blacks were literate in 1866. But by 1943, as Henry Bullock wrote in *The History of Negro Education in the South* (1967), literacy had risen to more than 80 percent among blacks who had attended school.

The Phonics Backlash

But if phonics was the reigning practice, its emphasis on repetition and drill was rejected by the most influential philosophers of education. Horace Mann, Massachusetts's secretary of education in the mid-1800s, wrote: "it is upon this emptiness, blankness, silence and death, that we compel children to fasten their eyes; the odor and fungeousness of spelling book paper; a soporific effluvium seems to emanate from the page, steeping all their faculties in lethargy." Mann preferred a method of teaching called "look and say," based on the ideas of Thomas Gallaudet, who was developing reading programs for the deaf. The premise of this method was that children could learn to read by associating words with pictures. Drills in letter/sound correspondences were unnecessary.

The father of progressive education, John Dewey of Teachers College at Columbia University, became one of the chief proponents of the "look and say" philosophy. In his 1898 essay "The Primary-Education Fetish," Dewey wrote, "The plea for the predominance of learning to read in early school life because of the great importance attaching to literature seems to me a perversion." Dewey believed that teaching children to read with phonics was drudgery that would turn them off from genuine learning.

In the early 20th century, "progressive education" and its attendant "whole word" or "look and say" theory of reading instruction spread to the teacher training schools, then called Normal Schools. But one of the paradoxes of a teaching philosophy designed to encourage intellectual curiosity and independence is that it limited children to a simplistic and boring vocabulary: "Frank had a dog," "See Spot run." The spoken vocabulary of most children at the end of the fourth grade exceeds 15,000 words. By contrast, the typical whole-word reading series taught children to memorize only 1,500 words by the end of the fourth grade.

Beginning in the 1960s, Ken Goodman, Frank Smith, and a bevy of "new Deweyites" promoted a reading philosophy called "whole language," which also avoided phonics. Whole-language theorists believe that children learn to read the same way they learn to speak. Teachers are taught that children are born with the ability to read, and all that is required is to surround them with books, read to them, and then let them read themselves, using context, pictures, and the beginning and ending letter sounds of words to guess their meaning. Ken Goodman, one of America's more famous whole-language advocates, writes in the *Whole Language Catalogue*, "Whole language classrooms liberate pupils to try new things, to invent spellings, to experiment with a new genre, to guess at meanings in their reading, or to read and write imperfectly. In whole language classrooms risk-taking is not simply tolerated, it is celebrated."

For the past decade, whole language has dominated the curricula of all 50 states, as well as the leading remedial tutorial programs such as "Reading Recovery," which has been endorsed by First Lady Hillary Rodham Clinton in her book, *It Takes a Village*. Whole language has been the central principle of reading instruction in virtually all teacher training schools, as well as professional organizations such as the International Reading Association and the National Council of Teachers of English.

The Research Is In

The great tragedy of all this is that research in reading instruction shows conclusively that whole language does not work, and that phonics-based instruction does. The National Institute of Child Health and Human Development (NICHD), a division of the federal National Institutes of Health, has funded and overseen empirical, replicable research at eight major universities (Yale, Johns Hopkins, Florida State, Bowman Gray School of Medicine, and the universities of Toronto, Colorado, Houston, and Miami) that has been reported in more than 2,000 refereed journal articles since 1965. The results of this research were summarized by Benita Blachman, a professor of education at Syracuse University, in a 1994 literature review published in *Reading and Writing: An Interdisciplinary Journal*:

"We have had a scientific breakthrough in our knowledge about the development of literacy. We know a great deal about how to address reading problems—even before they begin.... The tragedy is that we are not exploiting what we know about reducing the incidence of reading failure. Specifically, the instruction currently being provided to our children does not reflect what we know from research.... Direct, systematic instruction about the alphabetic code is not routinely provided in kindergarten and first grade, in spite of the fact that at the moment this might be our most powerful weapon in the fight against illiteracy."

In February 1997 Bonnie Grossen, a research associate at the College of Education at the University of Oregon, summarized the NICHD research and identified seven steps for producing independent readers (see page 100).

Empirical scientific evidence for the effectivess of phonics stands in stark contrast to the unvalidated whole language philosophy. Keith Stanovich, a well-respected researcher at the University of Toronto, wrote in the *Reading Teacher* (January 1994): "That direct instruction in alphabetic coding facilitates early reading acquisition is one of the most well-established conclusions in all of behavioral science. Conversely, the idea that learning to read is just like learning to speak is accepted by no responsible linguist, psychologist, or cognitive scientist in the research community."

> *"The phonics students scored 42 percentile points higher in reading overall, and 34 points higher in comprehension."*

At the 1997 meeting of the American Association for the Advancement of Science, Barbara Foorman, an educational psychologist at the University of Houston, presented a comparison study of two groups of low-income first- and second-graders who had been classified as "reading disabled." These students scored at the 25th percentile in reading ability at the beginning of the year. At the end of the year, the students taught whole-language achieved mean scores near the 25th percentile. Those taught systematic phonics had mean scores at the 43rd percentile.

According to Foorman, "such results suggest that direct instruction in sound-spelling patterns in first- and second-grade classrooms can prevent reading difficulties in a population of children at-risk of reading failure."

In 1985, Arizona's Peoria Unified School District compared the Spalding Program, a phonics-based language-arts system, with the district's existing whole-word program. Kindergarten through third-grade classes were paired in one high-income, two middle-income, and two low-income schools. By the end of one year, control schools' average reading comprehension scores remained at or below the 50th percentile, while scores from all the phonics schools at all incomes ranged from the upper 80th to the high 90th. Based on that evidence, the district adopted Spalding in all 18 of its schools. During the next eight years, Peoria consistently maintained scores 20 to 30 percentile points higher than neighboring districts with school populations of similar income.

Jane Hodges, a professor of education at the Mississippi University for Women, has compared first-graders in Aberdeen, Mississippi, who were taught in systematic phonics with those instructed in whole language. The phonics students scored 42 percentile points higher in reading overall, and 34 points higher in comprehension.

Such research results are beginning to affect teacher training. Columbia's Teachers College, John Dewey's home territory, has reintroduced systematic phonics in the curriculum for special-education teachers. Associate professor Judith Birsh teaches a course in alphabetic phonics that is now a requirement for completion of the Learning Disability Masters Degree program.

In the summer of 1995, the American Federation of Teachers devoted an entire issue of its magazine *American Educator* to the teaching of reading and the virtues of phonics. In one article, Maggie Bruck, an associate professor of psychology and pediatrics at McGill University, in Montreal, said she has "reviewed the entire database of educational research and [has] not found a single example published in a major peer-reviewed journal that showed that whole language worked."

The Reading Recovery program, which typically costs an astronomical $8,000 to $9,000 per student, has come under fire in five major research studies. As summarized by Bonnie Grossen and Gail Coulter of the University of Oregon and Barbara Ruggles of Beacon Hill Elementary School, these studies found that "Reading Recovery does not raise overall school achievement levels.... Research-based alternative interventions are more effective than Reading Recovery...and far fewer students than claimed actually benefit from Reading Recovery." Columnist Debra Saunders has written in the *San Francisco Chronicle*, "Reading Recovery—a program designed to prevent reading failure—is to education what the $600 toilet seat was to the military. Except that no one ever said the $600 toilet seat didn't work as promised."

Most Americans are unaware of what has been called "the phonics wars," but they are nonetheless taking matters into their own hands. Many are astonished that there is any debate about how to teach children to read. During the past decade, more and more parents have been teaching their children to read before they enter school or after schooling begins. Products like "Hooked on Phonics," "The Phonics Game," "Sing, Spell, Read, and Write," "Action Reading," "Phonics Pathways," "Alpha Phonics," "Saxon Phonics" and many others have taken the country by storm. Reports from satisfied parents are overwhelming. Millions of children are becoming proficient readers using these programs at home. Most of these programs are priced at a fraction of the costs of Reading Recovery, yet they work far better. Does it occur to any teachers that the same tools could be used in every kindergarten and first-grade classroom?

During the past several years, California, Ohio, Texas, North Carolina, Wisconsin, Virginia, Washington, have passed legislation that requires systematic instruction in phonics. Others are following suit. In 1997, New York, West Virginia, South Carolina, Nebraska, Nevada, Massachusetts, Tennessee, Mississippi, have similar legislation pending. While President Clinton fiddles, state legislators are finally listening to their constituents and taking action, and it is about time.

Meanwhile millions of students still suffer because of a disastrous teaching philosophy. Thaddeus Lott, principal of Wesley

Elementary School in Houston, Texas, and a leading authority on African-American education, commented recently: "When students are brought up on the [whole language] system and see an unfamiliar word, they are told to guess instead of decode. Frustration sets in when children are given a problem to solve without the means to solve it. Chronic frustration leads to negative feelings and anger and loss of self-confidence. That's not the way to empowerment."

There is a simple solution, one that was voiced by Rudolph Flesch in his classic book of 1955, *Why Johnny Can't Read*, and 26 years later, in *Why Johnny Still Can't Read*. "Any normal six-year-old loves to learn letters and sounds. He is fascinated by them. They are the greatest thing he has come up against in life." Teach the letters and sounds directly and systematically, and you will have lifelong readers who love books.

"'Chronic frustration leads to negative feelings and anger and loss of self-confidence.'"

Principles of Reading Instruction

1. Teach phonemic awareness directly in kindergarten. Students should be taught that spoken words and syllables are made up of sequences of elementary speech sounds. These skills do not develop naturally, but must be taught directly and systematically.

2. Teach each sound-spelling correspondence explicitly. Students should be explicitly taught the single sound of each letter or letter combination. Each day, there should be 5 or 10 minutes of practicing the sounds of letters in isolation. The balance of the lesson should provide practice in recognizing letter/sound relationships in decodable text.

3. Teach frequent, highly regular sound-spelling relationships systematically. Teach the students the 70 most common sound-spelling relationships. Systematic teaching means students should be taught sound-spellings before being asked to read them, and the order of instruction should progress from easier to more difficult sound-spelling relationships

4. Teach students directly how to sound out words. After students have learned two or three sound-spelling correspondences, begin teaching them how to blend sound/spellings into words. Show students how to move sequentially from left to right through spellings as they "sound out," or say the sound for each spelling. Practice blending words composed of only the sound-spelling relationships the students have learned.

5. Teach students sound-spelling relationships using connected, decodable text. Students need extensive practice in applying their knowledge of sound-spelling relationships as they are learning them. This integration of phonics and reading can only occur with the use of decodable text. Decodable text is composed of words that use the sound-spelling correspondences that students have been systematically taught.

6. Teach reading comprehension using interesting stories read by the teacher. Comprehension should be taught with teacher-read stories that include words most students have not yet learned to read, but which are part of their spoken vocabulary.

7. Teach decoding and comprehension skills separately until reading is fluent. Decoding and comprehension skills should be taught separately while students are learning to decode. Comprehension skills learned through teacher-read literature can be applied to students' own reading once they become fluent decoders.

Source: Bonnie Grossen, University of Oregon, summarizing $200 million in research conducted over 30 years under the direction of the National Institute of Child Health and Human Development.

The Oprah Challenge

Jeanie Eller is a master reading teacher from Arizona. One day, while watching Oprah Winfrey's talk show, she heard her remark, "Many parents do not know how to read, and therefore cannot read to their children." Jeanie issued the following challenge to Winfrey: "Select several illiterate adults, let me teach them for two weeks, and I'll prove that illiteracy in America is a fraud." Her challenge was accepted, and in February 1994, Jeanie set up shop in a small classroom at Winfrey's Chicago studio. Her students: Alfred Carter, age 69, who had attended school for only two weeks when he was six years old and who wanted desperately to read his Bible; Paul Burde, 35, upper-middle-class suburbanite, who hid his illiteracy from everyone but his wife and mother; Alberto Mendoza, 32, who had graduated from high school with a diploma he could not read and was told he was clinically dyslexic and would always be illiterate; Paulina Gomez, 30, who dropped out of school in the eighth grade when she became pregnant with the first of six children. Gomez had lived on welfare and drugs, and her children had been placed in foster care. She had gone through drug rehab, and she wanted to learn to read, get a job, and regain her children.

After two weeks of intensive instruction using her own phonics-based "Action Reading Program," Jeanie's students were calling themselves "the four Amigos." The day before the taping of the Oprah show, Jeanie and the "Amigos" walked the streets of Chicago, reading store and street signs. They were like children, laughing and pointing. They went to an art museum where they read the labels under the great masterpieces. They ate lunch, and read the menu aloud. Finally, they went to the public library, where they each got library cards. They were pulling books out of the stacks and reading paragraphs to each other, giddy with delight. One can only wonder what their lives could have been if they had been taught to read in first grade.

Do-Gooders of the World, Unite![3]

While the attention of the nation was fixed on Colin Powell, President Clinton, and the three former Presidents here for the volunteerism summit, I headed a few blocks down the street for the "People's Summit," with featured guests Jesse Jackson, Dick Gregory, and Ramsey Clark. Now there's some real history for you. Presidents and four-star generals, they are as the flies of a summer. But Jackson, Gregory, and Clark—they are forever.

I never did find Ramsey Clark—he must have had prior protest commitments elsewhere—but there was good ol' Dick Gregory, angry and indignant. Angry at Clinton for chumming it up with "corporate America." Angry over the abandonment of the poor by Democrats. Scornful of this "sham" of a summit for rich do-gooders while the real problems in America went unaddressed. All those fasts over the years have left Gregory with an impressive air. With hair combed straight back, a grey, Biblical-looking beard, white shirt and black pinstripe suit, and generally manly bearing, he's a throwback from a time when protestors still looked dignified. These kids today in their open shirts, torn denims, and Nikes—what do they know about rabble-rousing?

Lucien Blackwell, a former congressman from the area, then rose to urge white and black people to come together—against corporate America. "Stop that race stuff," he implored. "It's a *class* struggle!" A local activist lawyer named Obu Fadeyibi called the summit a cruel hoax and a fraud and a distraction. "Somebody sits in board rooms and thinks this c— up! We'll have peace in our homes and in America when people are able to have jobs!" And finally Jesse, working the crowd beautifully: "I am...somebody!"

"Stop the violence!"

"Save the children!"

"Jobs!"

"Now!"

"I am...somebody!"

Class warfare, mass unrest, basic inequities, confrontation, Now!—I found it all very refreshing. It's nonsense, but hard, tangible, unprettified nonsense. The real stuff, with a little kick to it, and not a pale, perfumed imitation.

Over at the volunteer summit itself, you needed at every step to distinguish the volunteers from the summiteers. The latter seemed to bear out the Fadeyibi thesis. You could walk into most any conference room and hear things like: "...And so our goal and hope for the future is plan many more local and statewide summits like this, to *broaden* this great network, and to think not

---

[3] Article by Matthew Scully, writer in Arlington, VA, and formerly *National Review*'s literary editor, from *National Review* 49:32-3 Je 2 '97. Copyright © 1997 National Review Inc. Reprinted with permission.

only nationally but globally. Our goal and hope and mission is to build bridges and to link the dots all over our nation and our country. And my message here today is that there's a lot of cynicism out there, and we can *break* that cynicism, and we can do that only if we *build* that bridge and keep the promise..."

Somebody sat in some boardroom, at a meeting with fellow bridge-builders and dot-connectors, thinking this was really visionary stuff—and great PR. It's not enough for the corporate sponsors Gen. Powell was constantly calling upon to "give something back" to donate money to good causes and leave it at that. There must be a global strategy, a broad network, more conferences, and more speeches until cynicism has been broken once and for all. If this is the voice of corporate America, I'm with Lucien Blackwell in the class struggle.

Other summiteers could be heard holding forth at the inevitable "Plenary Roundtable: The Role of the Media." Sensing a great void in America, a dozen or so journalists had hastened to the scene to volunteer their opinions. "Volunteerism is the big story of the latter part of the twentieth century.... Volunteerism is *redefining* what news is...."

Walking from yak session to yak session, however, you could meet the actual volunteers themselves. There was criticism from conservatives to the effect that the summit was all fluff or, worse, an attempt to collectivize private volunteering. Well, no. Most of the people here were just the sort conservatives have been extolling forever, who volunteered long before their good deeds were "celebrated" and will keep doing so when they are not.

The highlight for me was seeing Bill Russell and Bob Lanier, the basketball greats, ambling by in the hallway. They volunteer as mentors for city kids, Russell since his retirement decades ago, and both seemed embarrassed to be here talking about it. The most inspiring person I saw was a 15-year-old named Amber Lynn Coffman, who got a presidential award for starting Happy Helpers for the Homeless in her Maryland hometown. In a video before the presentation, at a "Celebration of Service" gala hosted by Oprah Winfrey, we saw her preparing lunches for the poor, handing out blankets, and describing how when she was eight she saw Mother Teresa on television and wanted to be like her.

There were lots of Ambers here, and they are each, as Rev. Jackson might say, "somebody." No one seeing them in action left here feeling alarm at a coming collectivization. Humble admiration was more like it.

Leaving aside, of course, the sight of America's Happiest Helpers helping themselves to a good share of credit for all this. They never merely adopt causes, the Clintons, they absorb them until everything is soaked in sentimentality and self-regard. "I am here," declared Mr. Clinton, "because I want to redefine the meaning of citizenship." Prodded on by his incessant "challenge to look beyond ourselves," we now enter "the era of big citizen-

"There was criticism from conservatives to the effect that the summit was all fluff or, worse, an attempt to collectivize private volunteering."

ship." Mrs. Clinton's performance at Independence Hall, a
screechy summons to national mobilization, was incredible.

There is evidence that the practice of selfless giving actually
pre-dates the Clinton years. But then, no idea or virtue ever really achieves true significance until the Clintons themselves have
discovered it. And then, a new era. Time to "celebrate" volunteerism, redefine it, analyze it, coordinate it, have Maya Angelou
write a poem about it, maybe mandate and nationalize it. Having
already invented compassion, public ethics, bi-partisanship,
meaning in politics, and reinvented government, they have now
invented private charity. Now if they would only invent modesty.

Beyond Bake Sales: Christian Volunteerism Needs to Be Directed Toward the Deepest Hurts[4]

If the 1970s was the "me decade" and the 1980s the "decade of greed," some analysts think the 1990s is emerging as the "we decade." After spells of looking inward, then grabbing as big a slice of the pie as possible, Americans are rediscovering meaning in togetherness and giving to those in need.

That's wishful thinking, perhaps, but it is the hope of the organizers of the Presidents' Summit for America's Future. The April summit's goal was to mobilize 2 million volunteers by the year 2000 to help "at risk" children and to enlist the support of corporate America. The volunteers are to serve as mentors and models to children and youth, ensuring their safety and health, giving them the tools to succeed through education, and encouraging them to serve in their own communities.

The crisis among America's youth is acute: According to one report, 14.7 million American children (21 percent) lived in poverty in 1995, 2.1 million more than in 1989. Almost 10 million children (one in seven) have no health insurance, 3 million are abused every year, and more than a half-million teens belong to gangs. Teen violence, suicides, and pregnancy are all on the increase.

With such daunting needs, it is strange that the faith community was given a seat at the back of the bus en route to the volunteer summit, especially since more than half of American volunteers credit faith as their motive. Religious leaders were not at first included in planning the event, and when they were invited to join, the religious leaders involved felt marginalized by the political and business interests already engaged.

The potential for volunteering should not be overlooked. For example, an African-American young adult testified recently in my church that he was mentored by one of our members in his inner-city Sunday-school class when he was a child. He has accomplished more in life than he could have imagined otherwise, he said, just because someone saw potential in him that his environment did not allow him to see.

However, we should not assume that massive volunteerism can solve all our social ills (any more than big government has done). Mentoring programs can ameliorate the problems of children growing up in single-parent families, but it does not guar-

---

antee stable homes. Corporations can donate people and financial resources to charitable causes, but that does not create more jobs. Volunteerism cannot solve the systemic problems in public education or make health care accessible to all the poor—though volunteers in both areas make valuable contributions. Those goals demand social policies that make financial and human resources available to all, as well as nurturing homes and local communities that cultivate environments hospitable to learning and good health.

Volunteer America

"Less than 8.4 million of the 93 million Americans volunteer in 'human services.'"

Volunteerism and voluntary associations form a "hidden" component in American history, according to American historian Daniel Boorstin. Out of necessity, colonial and frontier Americans formed associations to do for each other what they couldn't do alone. In signing the Mayflower compact, the pilgrims pledged "to all care of each others good and of the whole by everyone and so mutually." From the first, we were a nation of givers and joiners.

In the 1830s, the French social observer Alexis de Tocqueville noted that the new American republic was marked by a spirit of generosity and a practice of voluntary association. A century and a half after Tocqueville, Princeton sociologist Robert Wuthnow has documented that volunteerism is alive and well in America, but that it has always paradoxically existed alongside an oftimes stronger impulse toward personal freedom and self-reliance.

Indeed, volunteerism lives on. According to a study by the Independent Sector, 93 million Americans volunteered 20.3 billion hours in 1995. This averages out to 218 hours per volunteer or 77 hours per American. "There's hardly a member of Congress that hasn't used that 93 million number," wrote Michael Gerson in *U.S. News & World Report.* But, as Pastor Eugene Rivers of Boston's Azusa Christian Community asked Gerson: "If there are really 93 million volunteers in America then why are our cities worse then they have ever been?"

In reality, Gerson points out, more than a fifth of those hours consists of "informal volunteering"—anything from baby-sitting for friends to baking cookies for school fundraisers. These figures also include volunteers at cultural institutions and those who serve on boards and committees. Less than 8.4 million of the 93 million Americans volunteer in "human services." The same pattern prevails in church where our volunteer hours are more likely spent in nurturing the church family and keeping the congregational wheels turning, rather than in outreach to the needy.

"Volunteerism, Christian-style, is much more likely to mean serving on the parish council or the vestry, not conducting Life Plan seminars in prison," says Roberto Rivera of the Wilberforce Forum. "In the current volunteer economy," he adds, "giving the Metropolitan Opera $10 million...is [counted] the same as using that money to help 3000 inner city kids attend private schools.

Changing that economy requires reinventing human nature and that's not going to happen." The seeming generosity of American people is often an expression of self-interest. In caring for others, we care for ourselves.

Human as We Want to Be

So why should people bother to help others? "Volunteerism is good for the soul, and it's good for the country," Vice President Al Gore said at the summit, and that is reason enough for some people. Who doubts the therapeutic and civic benefits of volunteerism? Psychiatrist Alfred Adler had this simple prescription for melancholy: "You can be cured in fourteen days if you...try to think every day how you can please some one." The real malady, said Adler, was a lack of connection to others.

Harvard professor Robert Coles, himself an inveterate volunteer, was forced to wrestle with his own motivations for service by the unsettling comments of precocious nine-year-old Ruth Ann. A student in the inner-city school where Coles was volunteering, Ruth Ann said: "Well, it's nice that you're here, but where did you get the idea, that's what we wondered. Did you hear something bad about us?" Having suggested he was there to meet some need of his, Ruth Ann said, "We'll try to tell you everything that we know." And then she added, "If you folks need any help, we could come and help, you know."

Our motives for serving others will always be mixed. But when Coles shared his misgivings about his own motives with Dorothy Day of the Catholic Worker Movement, she chided him, "If we were going to forbid hypocrites to work here with us, there'd be no one to do the work, and no one to do the forbidding!"

Service as Vocation

In spite of mixed motives, Christians must "be compassionate as [our heavenly] Father is compassionate" (Luke 6:36). Christian service should also be guided by these principles (borrowed here from Wesley Granberg-Michaelson, general secretary of the Reformed Church in America):

Volunteerism has its own intrinsic value. There is a fix-it mentality in the American drive to volunteer. But although faith-based social ministries are often more effective than purely secular ones—Christian drug rehab programs, for instance, have an exponentially higher success rate—we do not serve because we are effective. We offer service with no guarantee of a pragmatic outcome, doing it in the spirit of Christ, who showed love to many who ultimately rejected him.

God's love provides the incentive for volunteering. When LensCrafters provides 1 million free eye exams to needy children and Pillsbury launches a mentoring program, it seems like good business—savvy public relations. And when economic incentives are offered, such as college scholarships for youth who volunteer, one asks: Is it truly *voluntary* and is it truly *service* when

"'Volunteerism is good for the soul, and it's good for the country,' Vice President Al Gore said at the summit."

a reward is provided? Christians need no incentive to serve other than following God's lead in showing compassion for his world. This means suffering with others, just as God's Son suffered with and for us.

Christian volunteerism should be directed toward the deepest hurts and needs. Volunteering for youth sports, service clubs, and school projects are all constructive, social contexts for fellowship and community improvement. But specifically Christian volunteerism will be motivated by the compassion of God toward the world's deepest needs. When John the Baptist's disciples asked whether he was the Messiah, Jesus replied: "The blind receive sight, the lame walk, those who have leprosy are cured, the deaf hear, the dead are raised, and the good news is preached to the poor." One sign that the Messiah had come was that God in Christ was ministering to the least and the lowest on the earth.

Volunteerism is not a comprehensive social strategy. Volunteerism individualizes social problems by putting a human face on a statistical mass. But volunteerism only reaches individuals and most often leaves structures untouched. Volunteerism alone cannot ensure that basic human needs are met and economic opportunity is offered to all. Society as a whole, including private and public sectors, along with the church, has a responsibility to work toward equal opportunity.

John Carr, social-policy adviser to the U.S. Catholic Bishops, received a call from a reporter on the eve of the Presidents' Summit. Now that LensCrafters and Burger King are getting on board with the call to volunteer, the reporter wondered, what is the church's response going to be? Carr responded, with irony: "I promise you, we will not stop doing what we've been doing all along now that others have joined the effort."

Service is what Christians do; servants is who we are.

Any Volunteers?[5]

In November, Colin Powell announced that his effort to "rescue" two million at-risk kids by the year 2000—all through volunteerism and private sector charity—was making headway, particularly when it came to encouraging mentoring. "This is one of our *major areas of concentration*," the former Gulf war commander said, motioning with his hands to show everyone just how much he meant it. But then Powell let slip that the private sector had not lived up to one of its most important pledges. Under Powell's plan, businesses were supposed to finance the bulk of a $10 million advertising campaign that would have allowed mentoring organizations like Big Brothers/Big Sisters of America to double in size. So far, corporations have supplied practically nothing, according to Catherine Milton, an official running the campaign.

The shortfall is, alas, emblematic of Powell's effort. Since kicking off his campaign at the presidents' volunteerism summit in Philadelphia last April, Powell and his nonprofit organization—America's Promise—have lined up 325 corporate "commitments" to donate money and employee time, all in the name of helping needy kids. But upon closer inspection, these commitments, cited by Powell in his report and touted by the media, sometimes turn out to be less impressive than advertised. For all of its good intentions, the effort by Powell and America's Promise may become a case study in the limits of private charity.

A major problem is that corporations favor their own pet causes, which often have more to do with imagemaking among consumers than with the needs of poor kids. "We found out very early on," says Diane Whitty, a chief fund-raiser for the mentoring ad campaign, "that corporations were not comfortable giving money for an ad campaign to raise more money"—presumably because there was nothing in it for them. Sears, Roebuck & Company, one company Powell cited, is sending 50,000 volunteers and needy kids—to see the circus. Powell also cited as an important commitment a promise by the John Nuveen Company to donate $80,000 in scholarships to Chicago public schools. But, according to a company spokesperson, the money is not targeted specifically at needy students. Every high school in Chicago can receive the $1,000 scholarship because, a company spokeswoman says, "we wanted every neighborhood that has a kid who's succeeded [despite an obstacle] to reward him or her."

This is not entirely surprising: as the trade magazine *Industry Week* pointed out recently, corporations frequently become more

---

charitable in order to erase their images as downsizing behemoths or to improve worker morale. For example, First Union Corporation has a literacy tutoring program that allows employees to spend four hours per month, on company time, tutoring kids. That sounds great; *Newsweek* even cited the program last spring. But the description is misleading. Workers can fulfill the pledge by tutoring the child of their choice—even their own kid—and they can even just go along on field trips with their youngster, according to company officials. Nickelodeon, the children's TV channel, pumped in $4 million per year extra for an ad campaign touting to kids the merits of volunteering. Of course, says a company spokesperson, "being nice to your little brother" or "raking leaves for a neighbor" counts as volunteering.

"Nickelodeon... pumped in $4 million per year extra for an ad campaign touting to kids the merits of volunteering."

But if this predicament was not unexpected, it was one America's Promise was specifically established to avoid. America's Promise is supposed to check up on corporations and make sure they are really directing their efforts at needy kids. As the organization's officials admit, however, America's Promise has no systematic way to verify those commitments: the group gets its information from companies through a questionnaire. "I think you make a good point," says Raymond G. Chambers, a founder of last April's summit, adding that he will retain some social scientists to conduct a study.

This might have been averted if America's Promise had the muscle to channel companies' pledges to nonprofit groups that know how to use volunteers. Nonprofit leaders say it hasn't happened. "I've spoken with ten to fifteen nonprofit heads," says one nonprofit leader, "and they say, 'We didn't get any corporate connections that we didn't have before [the summit].'" "[S]ome corporations were naïve about what it really takes to help kids," says Marty Friedman, head of a national Americorps program.

The sad part is that in calling on Americans to volunteer, Powell has indeed tapped into a social force with some potential to do good. The private sector just can't mobilize it efficiently. Take the Big Brothers situation. "The number of phone calls coming in asking for mentors is seven times higher than the number of people volunteering to be mentors," Powell declared. That's why the ill-fated ad campaign was so important.

To be sure, Powell's effort hasn't failed completely. Many corporations say it has at least helped alert them to the need to help at-risk kids. And a handful of businesses, such as the Ronald McDonald House Charities and the Taco Bell Foundation, which set up specific programs for needy kids, deserve praise. America's Promise began as a sort of anti-poverty panacea, but in reality it's something else—an effort whose main impact has been on corporate philanthropy itself. Corporate involvement in helping at-risk kids isn't worthless. It just isn't enough.

Cutting Back[6]

In the Cash-Strapped 1990s, Government Is
Depending on Volunteers to Fill the Breach

Long before Paul Martin was first elected to the House of Commons in 1988, he was active in a variety of volunteer activities that ranged from fund-raising for disabled groups to membership in the human rights organization Amnesty International. So when he became finance minister in November 1993, it was only natural, says Martin, that he pushed cabinet colleagues and bureaucrats "to make damn sure they facilitate the work of community groups." One of his first acts was to arrange federal funding for a pilot project to help find jobs for disabled people in Prince Edward Island that had stalled, awaiting government approval for more than two years. And in two of his past three budgets, he lowered the ceiling at which individuals could claim greater tax deductions from their charitable donations. But despite those efforts, Martin concedes, his desire to help volunteers runs headlong into what he calls "one unshakable reality. The deficit affects everything that we do as a government."

Ask not what your country can do for you, but rather what it is prepared to encourage you to do for others. In the cash-strapped 1990s, that is the new mantra of governments at all levels, as reductions in spending and services mean that they depend like never before on volunteers to do the work for free that governments once did routinely. "There is no question that governments have to rely on volunteerism more than ever in a time of cutbacks, and that makes it absolutely essential that we do all we can to recognize the importance of volunteers," says Martin.

That desire manifests itself in a variety of ways. One of the most obvious is a formal recognition of the importance of Canada's volunteers. That is evident in the new Caring Canadian Awards that Gov. Gen. Roméo LeBlanc will present to 12 recipients, one from each province and territory, on Canada Day. In March, Martin took part in a ceremony honoring "outstanding corporate citizens"—companies that work with community organizations to hire people suffering from disabilities. And there are the Canada Volunteer Awards, which Health Minister David Dingwall presented to 23 men and women with long records of service to their communities at a ceremony on June 18. Said Dingwall: "Governments have only woken up in recent years and started to acknowledge the significant contributions that volunteers make."

But behind such ceremonies and cheery declarations lie sober-

---

[6] Article by Anthony Wilson-Smith with Brenda Branswell and Luke Fisher, from *Maclean's* 109:40-1 Jl 1 '96. Copyright © *Maclean's*. Reprinted with permission.

ing truths. Since the Liberals came to power in 1993, they have slashed spending virtually across the board to community and special-interest groups that have traditionally counted on federal funding. And over the next two years, they will cut about one-third of the $17 billion they give to the provinces in the form of annual transfer payments. That means, in turn, that the provinces will trim services and subsidies, as well as the money that they give to municipalities. Since many volunteer groups rely on money from all three levels of government, the effects can be devastating.

Still, many politicians argue that there continues to be a need to fund community organizations. Even in the Reform party, which supports deep cuts in government spending in almost all areas, some say the Liberals should think twice before cutting grants to community groups. Reform MP Keith Martin, a medical doctor who volunteers his services each summer at an emergency clinic in his riding on the southern tip of Vancouver Island, describes the present situation for volunteer groups as "a sorry state of affairs." Adds Martin: "The cuts are coming too fast. Stability is needed to plan for the future."

"As recently as 1993, the federal government spent an estimated $200 million a year funding interest groups."

Directly or indirectly, those cuts affect almost all Canadians. One of the great dilemmas is that Canadian governments are cutting spending and support programs precisely at a time when many people need them more than ever. With the onset of new technology and an unemployment rate that has hovered around 10 per cent for most of the decade, an increasing number of Canadians are confronted by career changes, unemployment and the insecurity that those situations bring.

At the same time, the traditional relationship between government and the country's citizens that economist Judith Maxwell calls "the social union"—the web of rights and obligations that the two sides share—is breaking down. In a recent report entitled "Building Blocks for Canada's New Social Union," Maxwell and her colleague Margaret Biggs suggest that the two sides need to jointly establish new definitions of their respective roles in society. That, in turn, suggests that individuals and groups take responsibility for some of the tasks previously performed by government.

Through the years, organizations catering to interest groups and often disadvantaged segments of society have relied on a combination of public and private funds, and volunteer efforts. As a 1989 federal government study of volunteers noted, their activities encompass areas "beyond those traditionally understood by that term (including) activities undertaken without pay for unions, alumni associations and self-help groups." As recently as 1993, the federal government spent an estimated $200 million a year funding interest groups. No precise figures are available on how much that figure has fallen since then, but federal officials acknowledge that across-the-board cuts have affected virtually all groups. Some of those, such as the National Action Committee on the Status of Women (NAC), have controversial and overtly political agendas that on occasion run contrary to the wishes and policies of the government. That has led to accusations from some NAC members that the cuts were politically motivated. But government cuts have also directly or indirectly affected nonpartisan causes that include refugee assistance groups, children's aid societies, programs to help immigrants adapt to Canada, and charity groups with religious ties that help the impoverished.

In the lean and occasionally mean 1990s, the reality is that almost every facet of society depends at least in part on volunteer efforts. At Ottawa's city hall, few people who take the popular guided tours of the premises realize that the person leading them around is a volunteer. At one park in the city, Georges Langlois, a 75-year-old retired military officer, spends an hour and a half each morning cleaning the grounds—a labor of love. He phones the city's recreation department every time repairs are required and it, in turn, provides them. Without him, the park would stay in disrepair because the city cannot afford a supervisor to oversee it. And in Montreal, when the city planned to cut funding at certain rinks three years ago, residents struck a deal: in exchange for maintaining the rinks, the city puts up the boards, freezes the ice and leaves material to maintain the rink. Volunteers now maintain 68 of the city's 174 skating rinks. Those are jobs that used to be the responsibility of paid personnel.

At the other extreme, under Ontario's ambitious and controversial workfare scheme, jobs that were once done by volunteers are now being handed to a new group: starting in September, 54,000 able-bodied welfare recipients will begin working for up to 17 hours a week as a condition of qualifying for benefits. Their jobs will range from cleaning parks to cutting grass, reading to the blind to assisting shut-ins. A similar program exists, on a much smaller scale, in Alberta.

Supporters of the plan, led by Ontario Community and Social Services Minister David Tsubouchi, argue that it will teach welfare recipients new skills and restore their sense of pride. But the program also raises questions that affect both those required to work and those they are supposed to serve. Will an elderly person or invalid feel comfortable knowing that the person attending to them is only there because they are required to be? Will volunteers, many of whom enrol in programs for pure enjoyment, derive the same satisfaction working beside those who are clearly unhappy at having been drafted to work? As workfare becomes more widespread, who will screen such workers to ensure that they are given appropriate work, and perform it properly? All those issues pose new problems for everyone involved, says Val Davis, a director of the Community Resources Centre in Kanata, Ont., which provides services and training to underprivileged people. Says Davis: "We can't just send anybody out. There are vulnerable people out there. We have to do police checks on our applicants. How can the Ontario government pro-

"Government cuts have also directly or indirectly affected nonpartisan causes...and charity groups with religious ties that help the impoverished."

vide safe service without similar checks?"

Workfare is one example of the increasing efforts of cash-strapped governments to maximize their resources. But, says Paul Martin, while that need cannot be ignored, governments must also take care not to lose sight of another fundamental notion. "Just as governments cannot operate without volunteer groups," he says, "so we must remember that volunteers cannot and should not replace the government in many areas." For both sides to function effectively, governments will have to remember to not just ask what volunteers can do instead of them—but also what they can do to help the volunteers.

IV. Rewards of Volunteerism

With all the discussion about who's paying for community service programs or what falls under the guise of simple responsibility, Section IV looks at the personal satisfaction and rewards of volunteerism. There is one common denominator throughout charity work that remains, and no matter what the reward, whether spiritual or moral, there are always some deserving people who benefit.

Garrison Elementary School in Washington, DC, has created a program called "Elementary Baseball." In a personal essay, Colman McCarthy from the *Washington Monthly* shares his insights from observing the progress of this program. One thing is certain, according to McCarthy: the program has had a profound impact upon its volunteers. They have developed compassion, a better understanding of the world beyond their front door, and a healthy skepticism towards the political leaders who allow social and economic injustice to persist.

The government can encourage more giving and more volunteering, according to David G. Tuerck from the *Wall Street Journal*, by modifying tax policy for those contributing to charity. The Presidents' Summit for America's Future, a major proponent of strengthening volunteerism, represented a mobilization effort to give communities the assistance they need. Many of the rewards that come from volunteerism are uplifting, however, Tuerck feels that Americans deserve an economic reward for what the contribute.

At the minimum security Jester II Prison Unit, between Sugar Land and Richmond, and southwest of Houston, TX, church volunteers work with prison inmates in a pre-release program, teaching them about proper morals and issues within society. In an article by Jim Jones from *Christianity Today*, a unique prison program called the InnerChange Freedom Initiative is described. It is a program that teaches Christian values through Bible study and mentoring. It is being funded by the Reston, Virginia–based Prison Fellowship International, founded by Charles Colson, and eventually 200 inmates may take part in the program, which was to continue for each participant for six months after release from prison.

In attempts to be more responsive to society's needs, students are given valuable out-of-class experience when working with people. In an article from the *Journal of Higher Education*, students respond to a survey on volunteerism and involvement with community service. Students describe how volunteer work has affected them and changed their perspectives on humanity. Students were able to see their community service not as a burden, but as an enlightening experience through which they found out more about themselves. "A significant learning experience associated with community service was the opportunity to better understand the lives students worked to serve," concludes the author.

Lawyers often benefit disproportionately from successful communities and volunteer work in terms of professional growth and development, according to Gerald L. Bepko, whose speech is reprinted here from *Vital Speeches of the Day*. Therefore, they should provide leadership in "making voluntary contributions for the public good." Bepko, vice president for long range planning and chancellor of Indiana University, discusses the way in which lawyers should become involved in volunteer work. In return, Bepko says, "increased volunteerism should help [the legal] profession not only by making our communities more successful, but by helping to repair a somewhat tarnished image that lawyers have developed over the last generation or two."

Natural disasters can come upon any community rather quickly. More times than not the courage and effort of volunteers saves many lives. An article titled "Red River Courage" from *Maclean's* describes one family's effort to fight the flooded Red River, which generated a huge 2,000 sq. km. inland sea, stretching 110 km. from the U.S. border to the southern suburbs of Winnipeg. The family discusses the flood's impact on the community. More than 650,000 residents escaped the flood, for which they owe a large debt of gratitude to the civilian volunteers who had hastily built secondary dikes inside the fortified city.

Proper management and leadership ensure more competent, satisfied volunteer workers and organizational members, including those volunteers doing relatively unskilled jobs. This compilation ends with an excerpt from *Leading Without Power: Finding Hope in Serving Community* by Max De Pree, who explains how volunteerism generates hope and benefits both the individual and the organization in many ways. The inner strength that results from challenging oneself often results in an ability to pass that strength on to others. So, with better attendance at, and more active participation in, group meetings and events, nonprofit employees or volunteers could, in turn, provide a better interpretation of the agency's aims and activities and thereby improve the organization's products and services.

A Win-Win Situation[1]

The Real Benefits of Volunteerism

On the eve of the national summit on volunteerism in Philadelphia, A. Franklin Burgess Jr., a District of Columbia Superior Court judge, traveled to Frederick, Md., with Anthony Taylor, a sixth grader at Garrison Elementary School in the Shaw neighborhood of Washington. Burgess has been mentoring the youngster for the past three years. On this spring evening, the judge and the student took in the Class-A Carolina League contest between the Frederick Keys and the Wilmington Blue Rocks. That was the first treat for Taylor. The second came after the game when he and Burgess went to a restaurant for dinner with a friend who brought along some players from the Keys and Blue Rocks.

What Bill Clinton, Colin Powell, George Bush and assorted other exhorters to goodness were preaching in Philadelphia, Judge Burgess was practicing. And it should be noted that writing of his involvement in the life of Anthony Taylor is more than another exercise in journalism for me. The program in which they participate is Elementary Baseball, a non-profit venture that my son John McCarthy started four years ago after a stint in the minor leagues.

In 1993, John, who attended public schools from first grade through college, gave a motivational talk at Garrison Elementary. He told stories about Satchel Paige and Hank Aaron—both went to the same grade school in Mobile—and encouraged the Garrison kids to be the best baseball players they could be.

Baseball? they asked. What's that?

Few had ever played. For poor inner city kids, baseball is unaffordable: Families have little money for gloves, balls, bats. Then too, what families? Baseball is a game passed from fathers to children. More than 90 percent of Garrison's students live in fatherless homes. Many are raised by grandmothers.

John was invited by the Garrison principal to organize a baseball program. In a year, the school was the only one in the District with its own team. At the first practice, kids had to be told to run the bases counter-clockwise. They called runs "points."

If baseball was foreign to many, so also was literacy and the habit of reading. Few had an adult who pushed them educationally outside the classroom. Most males in the lives of these children were failures: relatives in prison, drug abusers, layabouts.

After teaching the Garrison children that first base was to the right, not left, John expanded Elementary Baseball into a litera-

[1] Article by Colman McCarthy, director of the Center for Teaching Peace, a Washington non-profit that supplies teachers and information to schools wanting courses on nonviolence, from the *Washington Monthly* 29:34-6 Je '97. Copyright © 1997 The Washington Monthly Company, Washington, DC. Reprinted with permission.

cy program. To be on the baseball team—Garrison now has six—the kids also had to attend an afterschool reading program where they were matched with a mentor and a tutor. To find the mentors, John turned to Chief Judge Eugene Hamilton of the Superior Court. John offered a simple, but persuasive case for why members of the court bench should come to the bench at the ballfield: Get into the lives of at-risk kids now in a positive way as mentors, he argued, or you may be in their lives in 10 or 15 years in a negative way as you're dispatching them off to jail.

At Hamilton's urging, judges and other members of the court heeded the call. By the time of the Philadelphia summit, Elementary Baseball—supported by foundation and federal funds—was matching more than 60 adults from the court with Garrison children.

Frank Burgess, Princeton '65 and Harvard Law '71, with two years of the Peace Corps in between, has been mentoring Anthony Taylor for three years. There have been lunch dates in the judge's chambers, at least two outings a month, and regular attendance at Anthony's baseball games.

"The goal is to recruit more than one million literacy volunteers for elementary school students to ensure that every child learns to read."

Burgess, who is the presiding judge in the court's criminal division and who oversees cases in which up to 90 percent of the defendants are young black males from the kind of neighborhood where Garrison Elementary is located, says he has seen improvement in Anthony's self-control: fewer tantrums during games, fewer outbursts at umpires. Though not immediately measurable, apart from the rise in his scores on national reading exams, Anthony appears to be benefiting from his involvement in the program. I know him to be more sociable, less withdrawn. Still, there are no guarantees. "In volunteer work," Burgess says, "we're not dealing in solutions to large-scale problems. It's on an individual basis, one on one. We have to believe we're fulfilling our responsibilities if we help one or two people along the way....Within any culture, it's difficult to know who's going to achieve and avoid crime and who won't. Kids can come from the most poverty-stricken background and [not] have mentors like me and still...rise above it and...[not] commit crimes."

In addition to Garrison's mentor program, during the last school year, over 70 literacy tutors—primarily college and high school students—were working individually with Garrison children. In late March, the President and Hillary Clinton spent a morning at the school, advancing what is part of the administration's proposed $2.7 billion "America Reads Challenge." The goal is to recruit more than one million literacy volunteers for elementary school students to ensure that every child learns to read.

Will it happen? After four years of observing Elementary Baseball close-up and recruiting tutors from my peace studies classes at Bethesda-Chevy Chase High School, the University of Maryland, and Georgetown University Law Center, I can report this about mentoring and literacy volunteerism: We can be more certain about the benefits it gives to the service providers than those it brings to the service receivers.

An Ulterior Motive

One of the main reasons that I've been pushing my students to get out of the classrooms and into the lives of people in pain is to lessen the intellectual damage that we teachers do to our students. We are so intent on cramming theories and abstractions into their heads that they leave us idea-rich but experience-poor. Be smart, be brainy, we tell them: Make A's in school and you are predestined to make A's in life. We lie to the students.

To correct the problem of experience-poverty, I've been sending students to Garrison and Elementary Baseball for the past four years. What they learn through service is a way of tying ideas in the head to actions of the heart.

The benefits are as obvious as they are unsentimental, even if the way my students express themselves is still tentative. Sarah Heard, one of my Bethesda-Chevy Chase seniors now doing well at Amherst, wrote last year of working with a child at Garrison: "I definitely gained a great amount from this experience. It was sad to have it end. It has given me an inspiration to follow up on tutoring activities after high school. I gained an enormous amount from the teachers at Garrison as well. Those who stayed after school to tutor genuinely cared for their students. The experience opened up a whole new area for me, and perhaps I will go into teaching in the future."

Dilshad Husain was in my University of Maryland honors class in the fall semester of 1996. One of eight students who became involved with Elementary Baseball, Dilshad was paired for 14 weeks with a boy named Anthony Brown. She described him as "dynamic, smart and smart-mouthed, fun-loving and handsome."

"I *may* be helping him," Dilshad wrote at the end of the semester. "I may be helping him to improve his reading skills. I may be teaching him a modicum of patience. I may be showing him that higher education is a thing to strive for. I may be teaching him that mental solutions are better than physical ones. I may be changing some stereotypes for him—that Spanish people aren't the only ones to play soccer! I may be teaching him how the world is enlarged through books. I may be doing a lot of things for him, intentionally and unintentionally. I am aware of this, and I know he is happy to see me every week because of these things and more."

"But I don't think he realized his gift to me. I don't think he knows how much he is helping me. It's a 'may' when it comes to my helping him. I won't know if I have done any long-term good for a while. But it is an 'is' when it comes to him helping me. I can see and feel everyday how I have been changed by him—the way he reacts to things and the way he sees things. He may not know yet that this tutoring is a two-way street, but I aim to correct that. Anthony Brown needs to know that he has a gift, and I am glad and grateful that he is giving it to me."

The after-school reading tutor for Anthony Taylor last fall was Eric Speigel from my Maryland class. His experience was much less smooth than that of his schoolmates. Anthony often came late to tutoring, let himself be distracted, and preferred to talk about sports. Sometimes, Eric Speigel wrote:

> I left Garrison feeling that I was wasting my resources. There were so many other kids that I had gotten to know and like. Why wasn't I with one of them? But on this roller coaster ride, next week could be a great one. Dedication entails commitment through the good and bad.... At times, I've wished I could be with one of those cute little kids that shower their tutors with affection and excitement every time they see them. I could take pictures, show them to my friends at school and say 'Here's my little buddy.' I'm sure there are many advantages to an experience like that. There have been times when I've wondered if I could have made a bigger difference [if paired] with someone who accepted and appreciated my efforts. Still, I wanted and received a realistic experience.... These kids need someone who will be there for them week in and week out. Whether they show their appreciation is irrelevant. After all, we are here to fill one of the many voids in their lives and satisfy their needs, not worry about [our] own needs. In filling some of the potholes and pitfalls in their own road to the future, we can only hope that it will one day be as smooth a ride as our own.

"The current military budget is 17 times greater than the combined spending of the six nations...we are instructed to worry about."

The current debate about teaching values in school might be resolved if more schools demanded community service and service learning programs. Only one state—Maryland—does. Students given chances to care for the victims of economic and social injustice will likely develop a value system that questions the people in power who let that injustice persist. That's risky. It's how revolutionaries get started, it's how a few teachers begin to wake up and realize the truth of Martin Luther King Jr.'s call: "We must encourage creative dissenters.... We must demonstrate, teach, and preach, until the very foundations of our nation are shaken."

Ironically, the gang of exhorters on the platform at the Philadelphia volunteerism summit—Clinton, Powell, Bush, Ford—are among those of one generation who helped create the mess and despair that the creative dissenters of the next generation are now called on, as altruists and idealists, to ease. Colin Powell was a ranking part of the Pentagon establishment that saw the United Sates bankrupt itself through military spending. The $700 million a day that Congress gives the Pentagon is three times what the Peace Corps spends in a year. The current military budget is 17 times greater than the combined spending of the six nations—North Korea, Iran, Iraq, Syria, Libya, and

Cuba—we are instructed to worry about.

Is there no linkage between the money wasted on militarism and the money now wanted for social uplift? I don't recall Powell decrying this squandering of the nation's wealth, neither while wearing his uniform nor in his autobiography detailing the glories of his career. Now he preens about as the savior of Generation X: "Let's volunteer together to take care of our youth and help shape America's future."

No. Reshape it. What's getting underway now in the literacy programs is catch-up work that wouldn't have been necessary if the country hadn't been impoverished by the military spending binge. Jimmy Carter administered a trillion dollar military budget, yet now he troops around the globe as Mr. Peacemaker. Powell gets away with his Mr. Volunteerism number, thanks to a fawning media.

Before enticing high school and college kids to cure the ills of society, those doing the enticing could use some instruction on accountability. That, too, would be one of the benefits of volunteerism, available to both servers and served.

America's Volunteers
Deserve a Tax Break[2]

Thousands of Americans have gathered for the Presidents' Summit for America's Future to find ways to provide health and educational assistance for children and to strengthen volunteerism and community values.

It is one thing to extol the virtues of volunteering. It is another, however, to apply volunteer effort effectively to solve America's problems. Doing so means taking advantage of the connections among tax policy, giving and volunteering.

We are a nation of givers. According to the most recent data, individual Americans donate more than $105 billion annually to charity; 22 million Americans give at least 5% of their income to charitable and community-based organizations.

We are also a nation of volunteers. According to Independent Sector, about 50% of Americans volunteer their services, to a wide range of nonprofit organizations. Twenty-five million Americans volunteer five or more hours per week. In total, Americans volunteer more than 20 billion hours per year. Valued at the minimum wage, this amounts to about $100 billion in volunteer effort each year, about as much as individuals contribute in cash to nonprofit organizations.

Thus, giving and volunteering already play a vital role in America. But what can government do to encourage more of both? The answer lies in part with tax policy. Consider the price that taxpayers face when they decide whether to give a dollar to charity. For an itemizing federal taxpayer in the 28% tax bracket, the actual price of giving that dollar is 72 cents. In effect, the federal government gives a 28-cent rebate for contributing each dollar.

The price of giving has a great effect on people's willingness to give and to volunteer, since the two go together. In his landmark 1985 book, *Federal Tax Policy and Charitable Giving*, Charles Clotfelter reported that people both give more and volunteer more as the price of giving falls. Most studies show that a decrease in the price of giving causes giving to rise by more than tax revenues fall. A Beacon Hill Institute analysis of more than 64,000 taxpayers shows that a 1% decrease in the price of giving raises giving by 1.12%.

Thus, the 28 cents in tax revenue that it costs the federal government to let a taxpayer deduct his dollar contribution to a soup kitchen is offset by a twofold benefit: The soup kitchen receives another dollar to spend feeding the poor. And it receives additional volunteer assistance from the taxpayer, allowing it to chan-

[2] Article by David G. Tuerck, executive director of the Beacon Hill Institute at Suffolk University, in Boston, MA, and chairman of the university's economics department, from the *Wall Street Journal* Ap 28 '97 p18. Copyright © 1997 Dow Jones & Company, Inc. All rights reserved.

nel more of its income directly to the poor.

If President Clinton wants to put substance into the spirit of voluntarism, he should recommend that Congress lower the price of giving by offering a tax credit—sometimes called a "compassion tax credit"—for individuals' contributions to charities that serve the poor.

A tax credit of this kind would permit the taxpayer to deduct part or all of his contribution to a qualified charity from his tax liability—rather than, as with a deduction, from his taxable income. Thus, Congress could reduce the price of giving a dollar to 10 cents by offering a 90% tax credit or to zero with a 100% tax credit.

While some might decry this as "tax tampering," it is in fact entirely consistent with a philosophy of limited government, since it motivates individual taxpayers to donate their own time and money to aid the poor and that reduces the pool of tax revenues available to government. The compassion tax credit is in fact the next logical step to welfare reform.

Indeed, the existing and widely used tax deduction is itself a form of tax tampering, and not a very democratic one at that. Fifty years ago, Nobel laureate William Vickrey condemned the practice of offering tax deductions as lending a "plutocratic bias" to giving. A tax credit eliminates this bias by giving the same price break to both low-income and high-income taxpayers, whether they itemize deductions or not.

"Some states already allow tax credits for contributions to charities that serve the poor."

Some states already allow tax credits for contributions to charities that serve the poor. A Beacon Hill Institute survey of nonprofit organizations in those states found that 87% of respondents believe that tax credits are a good idea. Eighty-three percent agreed that volunteers are necessary for helping those in need, 77% agreed that volunteers are reliable workers, and 88% agreed that volunteers save their organizations money.

There are a number of proposals before Congress to offer federal tax credits. These proposals represent a new kind of welfare devolution, one that strengthens those very community organizations for which the summit is a call to action.

The summit "is about getting Americans off the sidelines and getting on the playing field," says Colin Powell, its general chairman. The compassion tax credit represents our drive to get not just onto the playing field but over the goal line.

Unique Prison Program Serves as Boot Camp for Heaven[3]

Eighty-five Bible-toting inmates at a Texas prison are taking part in the nation's first faith-based prison prerelease program run 24 hours a day by an independent Christian organization.

The unusual experiment in church-state cooperation is the first time a state prison system has allowed a private Christian organization—Prison Fellowship International of Reston, Virginia—to take over an entire prison wing.

The goal of the round-the-clock volunteer program is to transform inmates spiritually and keep them from returning to prison.

"The InnerChange Freedom Initiative...is the first program of its kind in the United States."

"We want to change the inner man through the love of Jesus Christ," says pastor Don Bentley, a Prison Fellowship employee. "Until you do that, all you have is a polished-up convict."

The InnerChange Freedom Initiative—an intense blend of studying the Bible, teaching Christian values, and mentoring by church volunteers—is the first program of its kind in the United States. Houston-area church volunteers will work with inmates before and after they leave the minimum security Jester II Prison Unit between Sugar Land and Richmond southwest of Houston.

Rigorous schedule: Rising before dawn, the men make up their bunks inside their gray seven-foot-square cubicles. Each has a reading light. Some inmates display pictures of Jesus, crosses, or other religious symbols.

Encouraging signs are posted in different locations. "If It Is to Be, It's Up to Me," one message proclaims. Another states: "The Only Antidote to Pride Is the Grace of God."

At 5:30 A.M., inmates attend a mandatory worship service. Praying, hymn-singing, studying the Bible, learning life skills, and working at prison jobs follow. The day ends at 9 P.M.

Prison Fellowship, founded by Charles Colson, has allocated $1.2 million for the first two years to pay for programming of the pilot project and hiring of five full-time staff members. The Texas Department of Corrections is not out any extra expense, although the state provides the space, food, and guards.

Eventually, 200 inmates are to take part in the prerelease program. Groups are added in increments. Three sections have been received so far, and another group of 30 is due to join this month.

"Prison Fellowship wants to hike us up to 300 men, but the board will have to approve that," says Warden Fredrick Becker, a Methodist layman who has high hopes for the Christian effort.

The program makes efforts to teach basic virtues such as love, charity, self-sacrifice, honesty, and integrity. "Those things are

---

[3] Article by Jim Jones, from *Christianity Today* 42:88-9 F 9 '98. Copyright © 1998 Jim Jones. Reprinted with permission.

just words to most of those inmates," Becker says. "They've never experienced them in their own families."

Unlocking the good: On a recent morning, men dressed in prison whites and many carrying Bibles sang "Victory in Jesus," then listened intently as Pastor Bentley preached from a Bible spread before him.

"Many of you are here because of pride," Bentley said. "If you are a pompous and arrogant jackass, God is going to hold you accountable."

During a midmorning Lifeskills class, Jester II prison chaplain Jerry McCarty carried on the theme.

"This is a boot camp for getting into heaven," he said. "We want to unlock the good person potentially inside you."

Brandishing a Bible above his head, McCarty declared: "This is the owners' manual. Christianity is not just for old women and little children. It's for he-men, too."

Inmates who volunteer have committed a wide range of crimes, including murder, assault, drug-trafficking, embezzlement, and hot-check writing.

"If we had only altar boys and first-time offenders it wouldn't be a true test," Becker says. "I'm glad to say that the average man in the program is a third-time offender, and some are fourth- and fifth-time offenders."

Faith-based prison programs are gaining more acceptance across America, according to Reggie Wilkinson, president of the American Correctional Association.

"The Christian programs are more prominent in the Bible Belt," says Wilkinson, director of the Ohio prison system. "But prisons everywhere are letting faith groups in because of the need for the community to be involved in rehabilitating our prison population."

Changes evident: Some skeptics see the program as another version of "jailhouse religion," a term used to describe prisoners who seek easier prison time by embracing faith while behind bars, then toss their Bibles in the trash after they leave.

"A lot of people who have been in the prison system a long time just play games with religion," says Bentley. "They know what people want to hear and give it to them, but aren't really serious."

But the rigorous schedule of Christian activities weeds out those who are not serious, Bentley believes.

Patterned after methods that have sharply reduced recidivism in Brazil and Ecuador, the program aims to reduce the 48 percent return rate of convicts to Texas prisons. Statistical evidence on whether it is working will not be available for at least three years.

But the inmates, top prison officials, church volunteers of InnerChange, and veteran prison guards believe results are immediate.

"I've already seen changes in their habits and attitudes," says Sgt. Levi Peterson, 47, a prison guard for 13 years, who is not a part of the InnerChange effort. "When you get a group of inmates of different cultures and backgrounds to study together and read the Bible together, it's going to make a difference."

McCarty, the prison chaplain, concurs.

"We are stuck with anecdotal evidence now," he says. "But we see the look on their faces, the spring in their step, and the brotherhood that is forming. We see very definite changes."

Rough beginning: Walter Kasper, an inmate convicted of drug possession who became a part of the original group of inmates in InnerChange, says things have not always been harmonious among InnerChange participants.

"We had some real bad actors in our first group," he says. "We were a hodgepodge of 37 that stepped off the bus. Now our group is down to 20."

Many dropped out because they did not realize what a grueling schedule they would follow. Others were asked to leave because they could not adjust to the group environment and the rigid rules, Kasper says.

Texas Gov. George W. Bush strongly supports the program, one of several initiatives he has championed in which faith groups join with government agencies to help welfare reform, house the homeless, and help inmates after their release from prison.

Bush visited the Christian prison wing in October with Colson and joined the inmate choir in singing "Amazing Grace".

"Ultimately, inmates will be asked to put the brotherly love they are taught into action."

Ultimately, inmates will be asked to put the brotherly love they are taught into action. At the midpoint of training they will go out into the community, build houses for the poor, and try to apologize and make restitution to those they have committed crimes against.

No ACLU objections: A few groups, including Americans United for Separation of Church and State, have objected to the Christian program, saying it violates constitutional principles. But Texas leaders of the American Civil Liberties Union are not concerned.

"It follows all guidelines, and we have no problem with it," says regional ACLU director Diana Patrick of Dallas. "No one is coerced to be a part of it, and no special benefits are given."

Becker contends there is no violation because the program is entirely voluntary. Although Christian-based, it is open to all faiths. Two Muslims joined the first group, for example.

One Muslim, Joseph Williams, has converted to Christianity. But the other Muslim, Darryl Brown, continues to read the Qur'an and say Islamic prayers five times a day.

"They respect my faith," Brown says. "There are a lot of guys here who are truly sincere; and they are walking the walk and talking the talk."

About 200 volunteers are working in the program, but 350 will eventually be needed. Semiretired Houston attorney Jack Allen spends about 20 hours a week meeting with 14 inmates to evaluate their progress.

"After they get out we will continue to work with them for six months, minimum," he says. "They can come to us for help."

Allen says he cannot predict whether the program will succeed.

"We are just starting down the road," he says. "It will take more than my ability to change these folks. But if the inmates work with those trying to help them, it could be effective."

Judy Indermuehle, a real-estate agent and member of Sugar Creek Baptist Church who volunteers as a phonics teacher, had misgivings at first.

"Now I look forward to it every day," she says. "This is the church's first opportunity to affect prison life. And it's a wonderful opportunity."

In the Service of Citizenship:
A Study of Student Involvement
in Community Service[4]

Introduction

I learn more through my volunteer work than I ever do
in any of my classes at school. Talking to people from
diverse backgrounds provides so much insight that people just can't imagine. I study all these different theories
in political science and sociology, but until you get a
chance to see how the social world influences people's
everyday lives, it just doesn't have that much meaning.

I have been involved in volunteer work ever since I was
in high school, and I'll probably continue to do stuff like
Habitat [for Humanity] until I'm old and gray. I get a lot
out of working to serve others, and it's a good feeling to
know that I have helped someone even if it's in some
small way. It helps me to cherish people more and
understand what life is all about.

The preceding comments are from college students who discussed
their involvement in community service and the meaning they
derive from such activities. Both of these students give voice to a
form of learning that may be termed "citizenship education" in
that a concern for the social good lies at the heart of the educational experience. These students are reflective of others described
throughout this article who through participation in community
service explore their own identities and what it means to contribute to something larger than their individual lives.

In recent years, the role of higher education as a source of citizenship preparation has come to the forefront. In this regard,
higher education reflects a rising tide of concern for national service and the common good, as programs such as AmeriCorps,
Learn and Serve America, Habitat for Humanity, and Big
Brothers and Big Sisters have evoked our most prominent leaders as well as citizens across the country to commit themselves
to the service of others. The influence this national movement
has had on the academy is most apparent in the growth of organizations such as Campus Compact and Campus Outreach
Opportunity League (COOL) whose memberships and influence
increased dramatically in the early 1990s. Professional organizations associated with the academic enterprise also have added
fuel to the growing concern over social responsibility and citi-

---

[4] Article by Robert A. Rhoads, from the *Journal of Higher Education* 69/3:277-97
My/Je '98. Copyright © 1998 by the Ohio State University Press. Reprinted with
permission.

zenship. For example, in 1997 the call for proposals from the American Association for Higher Education Conference on Faculty Roles and Rewards specifically identified an interest in how community service and service learning contribute to a more engaged faculty. The 1996 Annual Meeting of the American Educational Research Association was organized around the theme of "Research for Education in a Democratic Society," and at the 1995 American College Personnel Association Annual Convention, one of the keynote speakers, Dr. Robert Coles, addressed the issue of moral education when he called for greater commitment to service learning and community service.

Although it is hard to argue with calls to foster social responsibility among our students, our future leaders, there also is a tremendous need for clarification. With this said, the following key questions offer a guide for addressing some of the confusion revolving around community service: (1) Are community service and service learning interchangeable concepts or are there important differences? (2) What is the role of community service in engaging students as democratic citizens in a culturally diverse society? (3) Are there variations in the structure of service activities which produce different experiences for students? The first question is examined as I explore the relevant literature on community service and service learning. The second and third questions are addressed primarily through discussions of the theoretical perspective, findings, and implications. Thus, the latter two questions form the heart of the theoretical and empirical analysis offered throughout this article. In weaving theoretical and empirical work together to address these questions, I follow the tradition of critical theory and support the argument that all research is theoretically rooted: Sometimes the perspective of the author is spelled out (as in this case), while at other times it must be interpreted based on the assumptions undergirding the work. This is by no means a rejection of empiricism in favor of theory, but instead should be understood as an effort to bridge the gap separating the two.

"For American colleges and universities a commitment to service 'is a movement whose time has come.'"

Community Service and Service Learning

Over recent years there has been an incredible growth in attention paid to community service and service learning. The increasing interest in service reflects to a large degree a concern that institutions of higher education be more responsive to society and that higher learning in general ought to have greater relevance to public life. A convincing argument could be made that for American colleges and universities a commitment to service "is a movement whose time has come."

The issue to be addressed in this brief review of the literature concerns distinguishing community service from service learning. The primary difference between these two concepts is the direct connection service learning has to the academic mission. Typically, service learning includes student participation in community service but with additional learning objectives often associated with a student's program of study. For example, a student majoring in social work may participate in service activities at a local homeless shelter in conjunction with a course of study on urban poverty. Specific activities designed to assist the student in processing his or her experience are included as part of the service learning project. The student, for example, may be expected to write a reflective paper describing the experience and/or there may be small-group interactions among students involved in similar kinds of experiences. The learning objective might be to help students interpret social and economic policies through a more advanced understanding of the lived experiences of homeless citizens. Seen in this light, service learning seeks to connect community service experiences with tangible learning outcomes. Assessing such outcomes becomes a central concern of research and evaluation.

Although service learning often is specifically tied to classroom-related community service in which concrete learning objectives exist, some writers suggest that student involvement in community service may be tied to out-of-class learning objectives and thus constitute a form of service learning as well. From this perspective, student affairs professionals who involve students in community service activities may engage in the practice of service learning when there are clearly articulated strategies designed to bridge experiential and developmental learning. The confusion between "class-related" versus "out-of-class-related" service learning led Rhoads and Howard to adopt the term "academic service learning" to distinguish the formal curriculum (largely faculty initiated) from the informal curriculum (largely student affairs initiated). Howard for example, defined academic service learning as "a pedagogical model that intentionally integrates academic learning and relevant community service." For Howard there are four components of academic service learning. First, it is a pedagogical model and is therefore to be understood as a teaching methodology. Second, academic service learning is intentional; that is, there are specific goals and objectives tying the service experience to course work. Third, there is integration between experiential and academic learning. And finally, the service experience must be relevant to the course of study. As Howard explains, "Serving in a soup kitchen is relevant for a course on social issues, but probably not for a course on civil engineering."

From an educational standpoint, it makes sense to link community service activities with intentional learning objectives whenever possible. Obviously, when student participation in community service can be connected to specific learning activities involving reflection, group interaction, writing, and so on, the experience is likely to have a greater impact on student learning and move into the realm of service learning.

In addition to varying degrees of connection community service may have to academic learning objectives, there are also differing opinions on which goals of higher education service ought to address. Whereas Howard stresses the role of service as a pedagogical model used to assist in course-related learning, others see service (community service and service learning) as a key strategy for fostering citizenship.

This vision of community service and service learning is captured most pointedly in the philosophical work of John Dewey, in which education is fundamentally linked to the social good and what it means to exist in relation to others.

Theoretical Perspective: Dewey, Mead, and Gilligan

This article is grounded in the philosophical work of John Dewey and his contention that education has a vital role to play in a democratic society. In his classic work *Democracy and Education*, Dewey argued that a democratic society demands a type of relational living in which one's decisions and actions must be made with regard to their effect on others. "A democracy is more than a form of government; it is primarily a mode of associated living, of conjoint communicated experience. The extension in space of the number of individuals who participate in an interest so that each has to refer his own action to that of others, and to consider the action of others to give point and direction to his own." Dewey's vision of democracy challenges all citizens to take part in a form of decision making that balances the interests of oneself with those of others. Democracy seen in this light demands that individuals understand the lives and experiences of other members of a society. How else can we weigh the effect of our actions if others remain distant and unknown?

Implied throughout Dewey's conception of democracy is an ethic-of-care philosophy akin to the work of feminist scholars such as Gilligan and Young, in which caring for others forms a core component of identity (often discussed as the "relational self"). This is conveyed in Dewey's view of liberty: "Liberty is that secure release and fulfillment of personal potentialities which take place only in rich and manifold association with others." Recent political theorists such as Battistoni also have recognized the importance of developing relational understandings of social life. For example, Battistoni supported Tocqueville's claim that American democracy is dependent upon "the reciprocal influence of men upon one another." For Battistoni, reciprocal influence is fostered through participatory forms of education, which he claimed are more likely to foster citizens who see themselves as active participants in the political process. Similarly, in discussing the relationship between citizenship and education, Barber argued that citizens must recognize their dependence upon one another and that "our identity is forged through a dialectical relationship with others." Barber calls attention to the idea that citizenship is fundamentally tied to identity.

"[Some experts] see service (community service and service learning) as a key strategy for fostering citizenship."

Mead and Gilligan provide additional insight into the connection between citizenship and identity through their respective concepts of the "social self" and the "relational self."

Mead's idea of the social self derives in part from James and Cooley, who both suggested that an individual's self-conception derives from the responses of others mirrored back to the individual. Mead argued that the self forms out of the interaction between the "I" and the "me." The "I" is the individual acting out some sort of behavior; the individual doing something such as talking, listening, interacting with others, expressing an idea. The "me" relates to the sense one has about the "I" who is acting out a behavior or set of behaviors. The sense we develop about the "I" derives from the interpretations we suspect that others have of us. We cannot develop an initial sense about ourselves without the help of others, who provide feedback and interact with the behaving "I." Through the imagined thoughts of others, we envision ourselves as a "me" as we become the object of our own thoughts. According to Mead, an individual cannot develop a sense of self without the interactive context of a social group or a community. Therefore, the other, either the particularized or generalized other, is essential to the development of the self.

Feminist theorists such as Gilligan also have developed a conception of the self strongly rooted in otherness. Gilligan was one of the first theorists to point out that women often make moral decisions based on a sense of connection with others. She argued that women's moral decision making reflected a fundamental identity difference based on gender. Whereas men tend to seek autonomy and make moral decisions founded on abstract principles such as justice, women, in general, seek connectedness and weight moral decisions based on maintaining or building relationships.

As a result of early child-parent interactions and ongoing gender socialization (which arguably begins at birth), relationships become central to the social world of women. For men, the relational quality of social life is often displaced by a strong sense of individualism. The other is fundamentally a part of women's experience and kept at somewhat of a distance for men. The development of the self for females may be characterized by connectedness. Male development may be characterized by individuation. These general patterns (which obviously vary in degree from one individual to the next) have significant implications for how males and females relate to others and how they understand themselves in the context of the social world.

Based in part on early feminist work, various scholars have argued that regardless of gender differences, society is likely to benefit when its members develop a commitment to caring. This is poignantly noted by Sampson, who argued,

> The feminist perspective should no longer be understood
> as developing a psychology of women but, I believe, is

better seen as developing a psychology of humanity tomorrow. The real issue, therefore, does not involve gender differences per se, as much as it speaks to an emerging theory of the person that is appropriate to the newly emerging shape of a globally linked world system.

Of course, Sampson's point about the "globally linked world" reminds us of an earlier issue raised in this article concerning how cultural diversity might influence citizenship education (recall key question Number 2: What is the role of community service in engaging students as democratic citizens in a culturally diverse society?). Arguably, as a society grows increasingly diverse, communications are likely to become more challenging. Cultural differences, though they may be understood as a source of community for learning and sharing among citizens, nonetheless pose a significant challenge to social interaction and an individual's ability to connect with the other, who, in the case of a heterogeneous society, is likely to be a diverse other.

Woven together, Dewey, Mead, and Gilligan, among others, provide insight into how citizenship education might encompass learning about the self, the other, and the larger society in which one exists. The "caring self" is the term I use to capture the synthesis of their work.

The caring self is intended to convey the idea of a socially oriented sense of self founded on an ethic of care and a commitment to the social good. Furthermore, it is reasonable to assume that community service, with its focus on caring for others, would offer excellent settings to explore the development of the caring self. But is this the case, and if so, in what kinds of service contexts are the qualities associated with the caring self likely to be forged?

This brings me to the crux of my argument and what I intend to shed light on through a study of student involvement in community service. Arguably, unless individuals have a deep sense of caring for others, it is less likely that they will engage in interactions with diverse others in a meaningful way. Caring may be seen as the solution to the challenge presented by a postmodern society characterized by difference. In essence, I contend that fostering a deep commitment to caring is the postmodern developmental dilemma all of education faces, including higher education. If we are to promote democratic citizenship in these challenging times, then we must foster in our citizens a commitment to caring. Higher education has a major part to play in this process, and involving students in community service may be one vehicle for meeting this challenge. The question that needs to be asked then, is, How and in what kinds of community service settings is caring to be fostered? Before addressing this question through a discussion of the findings, I first clarify the methodology used in conducting the study.

"Cultural differences...pose a significant challenge to social interaction and an individual's ability to connect with the other."

Methodology

The primary goal of this article is to advance understanding of community service as a strategy for citizenship education. Through a qualitative study of college students involved in community service, I shed light on various facets of the service context that may be most beneficial to challenging students as caring citizens. The focus is not on student learning per se; instead, I target the kind of meaning students construct about their service encounters as a means to identify important aspects of community service associated with caring. I need to be clear here. This article does not attempt to assess developmental change by examining student involvement in community service. Although such a strategy is important and falls in line with the tradition of student outcomes research, this article takes more of a phenomenological direction in which the essence of community service is the primary concern. Hence, the kind of experiences students describe are important in this study, not as learning outcomes, but as indications of the nature of the service context.

The data for this article were derived from research and participation in community service projects conducted in conjunction with three universities: Pennsylvania State University, the University of South Carolina, and Michigan State University. Community service projects ranged from week-long intensive experiences requiring travel to distant out-of-state communities to ongoing student service projects in the local communities or states in which these universities are situated. I participated as a volunteer in many of the service projects described throughout this article. My role ranged from a staff supervisor in a few cases to that of a graduate student volunteer with limited responsibility in other instances. In every case, my primary role was as a volunteer and not as a researcher; the data I collected was more of an outgrowth of the community service experience and was not the central objective. The comments here are not meant to shortchange the research strategy employed, but instead are intended to clarify for the reader the context of my interactions and involvement with the student volunteers. In fact, my role as a volunteer may actually add strength to the naturalistic strategies used in collecting data as I was able to engage in ongoing and meaningful dialogue with the research participants.

Based on the methodological strategies associated with naturalistic inquiry, data were collected using a variety of techniques, including formal and informal interviews, surveys, participant observation, and document analysis. The principal documents used as a source of data were journals students were asked to keep as part of their community service experience. The use of multiple data collection techniques provides a degree of triangulation and offers the researcher an opportunity to confirm or reject tentative interpretations.

The early phase of the study was conducted in conjunction

with Pennsylvania State University and the data obtained was part of a formal evaluation of community service activities by students. This phase of the project involved surveys of students' experiences and was considered program evaluation and as such did not require human subject approval at Penn State. The second phase, which primarily involved interviews and observations, necessitated gaining human subject approval. Students were informed of the study and given the opportunity to participate or decline. It was during this phase of the study that student journals were used, but only with student approval.

During the six-year period (1991–1996) in which data were collected, 108 students participated in interviews, 66 students completed open-ended surveys, and more than 200 students were observed at various project sites in which participant observation was central. Approximately 90% of the students involved in the community service projects were undergraduates, and about 10% were graduate students. The vast majority (approximately 80%) of the undergraduates were traditionalage students in the range of 18 to 24 years old. Females represented approximately 60% of the sample, and in terms of race, the majority were Caucasian (roughly 85%), with African Americans constituting the largest minority group—about 8 to 10% of the overall group.

Interview transcripts (from both formal and informal interviews), open-ended surveys, field notes from participant observation, student journals, and documents collected in conjunction with various service projects form the entire data base for the study. Once collected, the data were read repeatedly in an effort to identify important and relevant themes. The process followed the kind of analytical strategy stressed in the work of cultural anthropologists and interpretivists. Specifically, themes were identified based on their contextual significance and relevance to the overall goal of the project: to better understand the context of community service and how such activities might challenge students' understandings of citizenship and the social good. In a procedure described by Lincoln and Guba as "member checks," themes and interpretations were shared with several students as part of a process to obtain feedback and incorporate student reactions into the final manuscripts.

Based on the data analysis, several themes were identified. Three of those themes—students' explorations of the self, understandings of others, and views of the social good—form the basis for this article.

Other issues, such as "student motivation" for getting involved in community service and "attitudes toward community service," are examples of additional themes that emerged from the data analysis but are peripheral to this article and thus are not discussed in any substantive way.

"Themes were identified based on their contextual significance and relevance to the overall goal of the project: to better understand the context of community service."

Findings

In keeping with the theoretical concern of democratic citizenship and fostering more caring selves, the findings are organized around three general concerns suggested by students in discussing their participation in community service: self-exploration, understanding others, and the social good. These themes are highly interactive and, in general, students' exploration in all of these areas contributes to understanding what I describe as the caring self.

Self-Exploration

Participation in community service is an educational activity that lends itself to identity clarification. For example, a student who was part of an intensive week-long community service project in South Carolina talked about identity issues and her participation in the project: "I'm kind of in a search for my own identity, and this trip is part of that search. I just don't know quite who I am yet. I'm struggling to figure it all out. These kinds of experiences help. I'm most genuine in these kinds of settings." Another student added, "Getting involved in community service helps me to get back in touch with who I really am. It reminds me that I have more to live for than merely myself." A third student offered the following comments:

> I've always done service work. During my freshman year at USC [University of South Carolina] I worked on the City Year project and the Serv-a-thon. I believe service is an important part of leadership. It's important to give back to the community. The last four weeks I've been totally into myself, like running for vice president of the student body. I signed up for this project because I wanted to get outside myself for awhile.

This student saw the service project as an opportunity to connect with others and in her words "get outside" of herself. For her, the service project offered a chance to become more other-focused and to contribute to her community.

A second student described her involvement in community service as part of a journey to better understand herself: "My work as a volunteer has really helped me to see that I have so much more to understand about myself in order to grow. I'm still on the journey and have a long way to go." And a third student discussed what he learned about himself: "I got involved in volunteerism because I wanted to learn more about myself. I've learned how to love a wide range of people despite differences between us. I've learned not to be judgmental." A fourth offered insight into the kind of soul searching students often go through as a result of service work:

> Sometimes I feel like I'm only fooling myself and that I'm really only into service so that I can help myself. I list this stuff on my resume and I feel guilty because I know it will help me get a teaching job. Is that why I do this? I know

it makes me feel better about what I do in my spare time, but who am I really serving?

This student recognized, like others, the positive returns of service, not only in terms of experience helpful for landing employment, but for the feelings reflected back to the self.

Self-exploration through community service often involved a kind of self-interrogation that helped students to think more seriously about their lives. Listen to the following student as she recalled her volunteer work with troubled youth:

I got involved in a lot of self-esteem work, primarily with teenagers. It helped me to think more seriously about my understanding of myself and how others think of me. I began to wonder about what kind of person I was and was going to be. I began to ask questions of myself: "Am I too judgmental? Am I open to others? Am I sensitive to how other people see the world?"

Once again, the role of community service in challenging one's sense of self is clear. Equally clear is how one's sense of self is tied to the social context and the views others hold of us.

Understanding Others

A significant learning experience associated with community service was the opportunity to better understand the lives students worked to serve. Students were able to put faces and names with the alarming statistics and endless policy debates about homelessness as well as rural and urban poverty. As one student explained,

Expressing what it has meant to me to actually have the chance to engage in conversations with people who used to be total strangers is next to impossible. It has been eye opening. My understanding of homeless people was based on what I'd see on the news, in magazines, or on TV shows. They were not real people and I could easily turn my back on them and the problem in general.

Lawyers, Volunteerism, and Philanthropy[5]

Peace of Mind and Contentment

For the past 10 years, I've been away from law. I maintain my connection with the law school by teaching one course each year and by seeing some members of the faculty on my way in and out of the law building. My presence is regarded by my fellow law faculty colleagues only for a month or so before our budget discussions each year. Apart from that, there's usually icy silence.

This is exemplified by an incident that took place last year as I was driving downtown. To understand the incident, you must know that there was a time—about 15 years ago—when I was a member of a tennis group consisting of four of us law faculty members. We reserved two hours every Friday afternoon for doubles tennis. Toward the end of my membership in this tennis group, when I was dean of the law school, I was able to play fewer and fewer times each year. The last year I participated, I paid my $200 for my share of the court time and then played only three times. This means I paid $66 per game, and my colleagues beat me mercilessly all three times, since I wasn't playing very much in those days.

Now, I was driving past the law school on my way downtown to try to advance the case for a new law building. I was talking to a law alumnus on the car phone about why his daughter didn't get into the law class that year. As I was just approaching the law school, I saw four faculty dressed in tennis shorts, with tennis rackets in hand, walk out of the front door. Two of them were from my old group of tennis players of 15 years ago. Two of them were new faculty.

I blew the horn and waved. The two new faculty members don't know me and looked at me in bewilderment, probably asking themselves, "Why is this person waving?" The two senior faculty won't speak to me anymore, or regard me in any way, since they don't think I'm doing enough to support the law school. They responded with sullen indifference. They'd probably charge me $200 per game to beat me today, I thought, as I stopped waving and drew my attention back to driving and the angry alumnus on the phone.

Because I don't play tennis anymore, for the past 10 years, I've spent a greater and greater amount of my time as a volunteer. I've been on more than a dozen not-for-profit or volunteer boards; I've painted houses, done yard work, raised money for a

---

[5] Address by Gerald L. Bepko, Indiana University vice president for long range planning, chancellor of Indiana University, delivered on the Occasion of the American Bar Association Site Evaluators Workshop, Indianapolis, IN, on February 10, 1996, from *Vital Speeches of the Day* 62:463–465 My 15 '96. Reprinted with permission.

lot of good causes, as well as my regular fund raising for the university. This past year, I chaired the United Way Campaign for Central Indiana, and we raised nearly $31 million dollars.

This volunteer experience prompts me to want to talk to people who may have influence in the law profession—about lawyers as volunteers. I can't begin, however, by offering data on how much lawyers volunteer. There simply are no good data on this subject. There are data on how much physicians volunteer or give to good causes in the community, but there is nothing useful on the subject of what lawyers do. My impression is that it is not enough.

I also cannot talk about volunteerism or philanthropy as a method of generating business. This is something lawyers have done historically, although they may do less of it today because they are now allowed to advertise directly to the public. Also, I don't wish to talk about volunteering that involves psychological benefits or ego nourishment. Some boards are very prestigious. The board members get their names on the cornerstones of buildings. And some involve perquisites, such as tickets to football games or other highly publicized community events.

"Lawyers are facilitators—a part of the infrastructure for the success of a community."

What I would like to talk about are those types of volunteerism that involve some significant mixture of altruism—actions based on a selfless devotion to others or the society. I'm thinking of volunteer work based on commitment to causes, such as pro bono service in environmental matters or volunteer service in a hospital for children, such as our Riley Children's Hospital, part of the Indiana University Medical Center. And I'm thinking of acts that are based on some element of free choice. If your senior partner tells you, you should be a member of the hospital board, it's not pure volunteerism. The same is true if the senior partner tells you that, if you want to make partner, you had better become a United Way Key Club member.

I begin with some community-based considerations.

Law firms are service providers for economic communities. In general, law firms do not create wealth apart from the value that is generated in a business community. Lawyers are facilitators—a part of the infrastructure for the success of a community. This is not to suggest that lawyers are parasitic. They do create enormous value. It is to suggest that lawyers will more often flourish in healthy communities where there is economic growth, and will be less likely to be successful, over the long term (other than perhaps for a few bankruptcy lawyers), in a community that is not healthy, or in which there is economic decline. The success of a community (a state or a region) may be more important to lawyers or accountants than it is for some others, such as manufacturers. Manufacturers can more often or more easily address national markets, and still can do so (albeit less well) in a community that is itself in decline. Such a national market is not nearly as easy for lawyers to address, although there are a growing number of national law practices.

A good educational system, which produces a very good work force; a set of social institutions that limits poverty, good cultural institutions that enrich life; good human services that help people when they're in need; and good government that facilitates the pursuit of life and liberty; all these things contribute to good conditions for a law practice. Also, they attract high quality people, those who are more likely to create wealth. They also attract businesses. It is much more likely to find the ingredients for the creation of new business in a successful community. It is also likely that those businesses will be held in place in the community and won't move off like some professional sports franchises. It is also important in attracting and retaining company headquarters, something that is of great significance to lawyers and accountants and other infrastructure providers.

The quality of life—the educational, cultural, and human features of life in a community—have been supported by government at varying levels throughout our history. Today, we may be at the end of a period of most intense government involvement.

With respect to the redistribution of wealth and welfare, it is clear that there is fundamental rethinking under way, whether you focus on President Bill Clinton's commitment to change welfare as we know it in his campaign for the presidency in 1992; whether you look at Newt Gingrich's political tome, *To Renew America*; or whether you look at books such as Marvin O'Lasky's, *The Tragedy of American Compassion*. Wherever you look, it seems clear that there will be changes in the way we provide support to those who are less fortunate. Most of those advocating change have suggested that there will be more dependence on private philanthropic efforts.

More fundamentally, there is a movement to restrict the amount of gross domestic product that is consumed in government programs and payments of any kind. The federal budget balancing effort and an anti-tax mood in the states, seem to be moving us toward placing more emphasis on private volunteerism and philanthropy as the solution to community problems and for the improvement of each community's quality of life.

If this is so, it will be necessary for communities to create more of a volunteer or philanthropic spirit. My assumption is that, in a professional sense, lawyers benefit disproportionately from successful communities and should provide leadership in this effort. They should take the lead in being volunteers and making voluntary contributions for the public good.

Increased volunteerism should help our profession not only by making our communities more successful, but by helping to repair a somewhat tarnished image that lawyers have developed over the last generation or two. You've heard as much about this as I have, although as a reformed and retired lawyer I may hear more candid comments from observers about the problems of the legal professions. Today many laypersons view lawyers with unfocused resentment. This seems based on the assumption that lawyers take disproportionate value out of the economic system, not only in litigation costs but in disruption of legitimate business transactions and the employment of costly and needless defensive practices. Lawyers are blamed for what has been described as the strangulation of life and commerce through intricate regulation that leaves too little to the judgment and discretion of wise and prudent people. And the public, rightly or wrongly, thinks that lawyers are arrogant. More volunteer work and philanthropy by lawyers could surely address the perception of arrogance, and it could recreate the aura of selfless service that once seemed more a part of the foundation for the practice of law. I assume that this would be helpful for us as a profession.

There is also a moral dimension to our duty to the community. Don't we owe something to our communities? Shouldn't we feel a duty, if for no other reason than to pay back the benefits we've received? If you take into account the real costs of legal education, I doubt that any one of us hasn't benefited from the sacrifice of others. Even in independent universities, the cost of legal education often is borne in significant part by many who have contributed voluntarily and built up endowments or supported current scholarship funds. Those of us who attended independent law schools have benefited from the contributions of those persons of commitment. If you attended a public university, as I think more than half of us must have, then your education was supported in an even greater way by your fellow citizens. Depending on the public university, the total costs—I'm not referring only to direct costs, but the total costs of education—may have been supported to the extent of 40 or 50 percent by public funds. Shouldn't those of us who have been the beneficiaries of this type of support be called upon to devote part of our time and resources to the community that supported us? This is what commentators on philanthropy call "serial reciprocity" each person benefiting and contributing in serial fashion.

Lawyers are also benefited by volunteer activity in that there is professional growth and development. The dynamics of decision making—particularly in businesses—must be understood thoroughly by lawyers in order to do their jobs effectively. Volunteers become knowledgeable about how decisions on boards and in other organizations are made.

These decision makers are normally community leaders and potential clients. It may be important for lawyers to get to know business and community leaders in their natural environments and see them make decisions about matters of importance to them. Lawyer volunteers will also obtain a knowledge of how the community works and how different forces make communities more successful or less successful. These may be skills and insights important for all lawyers.

Also, there is an idea that has been advanced recently by Tony Kronman, dean of the Yale Law School, in a book titled *The Lost Lawyer*. He has argued that the law practice has declined in its

"More volunteer work and philanthropy by lawyers could surely address the perception of arrogance."

attractiveness and in its professional standing because we have lost the ability to pursue the ideal of a lawyer statesman.

Most lawyers hope that their work will be a source of satisfaction, in itself, and...be important...in their fulfillment as human beings. This belief is faltering, and there is a growing crisis of morale. Disguised by the material well-being of lawyers, it is a spiritual crisis that strikes at the heart of professional pride. It seems to be one of the contributing factors in so many lawyers experiencing burnout at midcareer and seeking other professional opportunities.

The crisis has been brought about by the demise of an older set of values at the core of which was the belief that the outstanding lawyer—the model—is not simply an accomplished technician, but a person of prudence and practical wisdom, something Tony Kronman calls the lawyer statesman. Kronman argues that we "...understood this wisdom to be a trait of character that one acquires only by becoming a person of good judgment, and not just an expert in law." This is deeply fulfilling as a kind of work and was seen as having intrinsic value.

The faltering belief is most evident in large law firms, which are much bigger than their counterparts of a generation ago and more likely to have multiple offices across regions. Their relationships with clients are more fluid and market-oriented, as are their relationships with their own lawyers, who now more easily move from one firm to the next. The work of these firms is more specialized; the lawyers who do the work are more likely to be organized into a series of specialized departments, orchestrated into a set of structural relationships between specialists in different fields and with different client bases, sometimes called a "cluster of marvelously stocked boutiques." The lawyers who do the work are more likely to be organized into a hierarchy of staff positions that include a large number of permanent, salaried employees who are neither partners nor candidates. Their average working day is longer than it was 10 years ago, and it continues to lengthen, although real income, measured by hours, appears to have gone down. While this forum is not a good one in which to try to unpack all of Kronman's ideas, it seems to me that the lawyer statesman is a model that includes good citizenship and public service. Developing the trait of character that one acquires only by becoming a person of good judgment is closely associated in my mind with the lawyer volunteer. It is also associated with personal fulfillment—something I'll return to in a moment.

This ideal for lawyering may be related to the organizational thinking that suggests that the best organizations are those that set the highest standards for integrity and service, including volunteerism. There is a growing belief that companies with "character" and with the highest standards of integrity and honor, are actually the most successful. The best people want to be associated with them. The best people produce the most successful environments and the best products, from blue jeans to legal briefs.

Consider the case of Levi Strauss and Company reported in a book by Robert Waterman titled, *What America Does Right*. Strauss was not a very successful company until its employees embraced a new company philosophy. I will read from Strauss documents: "We want a company that our people are proud of and committed to.... Above all, we want satisfaction from accomplishments and friendship, balanced personal and professional lives, and to have fun in our endeavors... [We want] leaders at every level who set, live and teach very high ethical standards." I should note that in the wake of embracing these ideals, from 1982 to 1992, the average growth rate in shareholder value for Levi Strauss was 50 percent per year.

But can an organization that has character, and whose members volunteer, really be a winning organization? Doesn't some of the emphasis on idealism cause organizations to be distracted less focused on winning and profit? I don't believe so. In fact, the opposite may be true. A good example is the one I've just cited— Levi Strauss and Company. But to reaffirm that point, let me use a sports metaphor that involves the Notre Dame football team in their 1988 championship season. Notre Dame was about to play the University of Southern California at home. Although Notre Dame was undefeated and ranked number one in the nation, Southern Cal was the favorite in the game because of the home field advantage.

"There is only one way to achieve a high quality of life; that includes service to others."

Tony Brooks was the sophomore starting runningback, sharing duties with Ricky Watters, who has gone on to NFL fame. The two of them had a habit of showing up late for team events. The night before the all-important game, Brooks and Watters showed up late for a team meal. Coach Lou Holtz concluded that their indifference was having an effect on the overall character of the team and, despite their crucial star status on the team, Holtz sent them home. The integrity of the football program was more important than their individual contributions. The two of them ended up watching the game on a television set at O'Hare airport.

The good news, that all Notre Dame fans will recall, is that Notre Dame won the game 27 to 10, without Watters and Brooks. Upholding principles and ideals can be, over the long term, more important in winning and in success, as measured by traditional terms, than ensuring that every ounce of energy is devoted to profit. By the way, Notre Dame went on to win the national championship with a bowl victory over West Virginia.

What may be more important than anything else is the personal satisfaction that is derived from volunteer activity. It is a defining element of life. Greg Petersmeyer, George Bush's "thousand-points-of-light" person, said when he spoke at IU some years ago, "The definition of a successful life should always include voluntary service." There is only one way to lead a full and rich life; there is only one way to achieve a high quality of life; that includes service to others. This lesson could address the dispiriting midcareer doldrums that are becoming more prevalent among lawyers, at least if my sampling of former students is representative. It also may set an important example for others, especially younger people who are developing their understanding of life and their professions. I often think that a good way of measuring whether our decisions are correct is by envisioning whether we would be proud to make those decisions in the presence of our children. A decision to help others would nearly always make you proud.

Over the longterm, over the course of a lifetime, there are few things that are as rewarding as the knowledge that you have made a good contribution to your community in a way that involves altruism, commitment, and sacrifice. Peace of mind and contentment that come from having made a contribution to make our world better, even in small ways, can be one of life's great satisfactions.

The late Robert F. Kennedy, then Senator from New York, said, "Too much and for too long we seem to have surrendered personal excellence and community values in the mere accumulation of material things. Our gross national product counts such things as air pollution and cigarette advertising...yet the gross national product does not allow for the health of our children, the quality of their education or the joy of their play. It does not include the beauty of our poetry or the strength of our marriages, the intelligence of our public debates, or the integrity of our public officials. It measures neither our wit nor our courage, neither our compassion nor our devotion to our country. It measures everything, in short, except that which makes life worthwhile; and it can tell us everything about America except why we are proud to be Americans."

On balance, I'd say that lawyers should make the time and accept the responsibility to do more for their communities. I have, and I'm profoundly pleased that I did and will have, I hope, the opportunity to continue. You should consider taking this message to the law schools you visit.

Red River Courage[6]

Ron Isaac's dark red pickup is parked at the end of a narrow country lane, right at the point where the roadway's greasy surface disappears beneath the wind-whipped wavelets of a coffee-colored sea. Inside the truck's cab, the 62-year-old Manitoba farmer and seed-grain dealer points towards a distant clump of trees, one of a dozen similar isolated islands of greenery rising from the roiling waters. "That's my place over there on what used to be the south bank of the Morris River," he says, matter-of-factly. "My seed bins are gone, water's up to the main floor around the house." He thumbs the brim of a battered baseball cap from his brow, leans an elbow on the steering wheel. "You know, I've lived in this valley since I was a boy, fought all the big floods," he continues, ticking off the particularly bad years—1950, 1966, 1979, 1996—on the fingers of one hand, signposts in a lifetime of struggle with the implacable power of the Red River and its many tributaries. "I thought I'd seen everything that old river could throw at me. But this one," he sighs, giving his head a single, tiny shake, "this one has been the great-granddaddy of them all."

The flood of the century, they have been calling it in Manitoba, an awesome demonstration of nature's raw might. In its relentless march northward, it spawned an enormous inland sea, a 2,000-square-kilometre fan of murky water stretching all the way from the United States border, 110 km north to the southern suburbs of Winnipeg. The Red flowed over 800 farms, inundating some of the richest soil in the country and affecting 10 of Manitoba's 14 federal ridings. Close to 25,000 residents fled their homes for higher ground, 8,000 of them in the provincial capital. A vast assemblage of machinery and a huge army have been mobilized to fight the menace, countless thousands of civilians as well as 8,500 soldiers, sailors and airmen from the Canadian Forces—three times the combined strength of the country's United Nations peacekeepers in Bosnia, Haiti and the Golan Heights.

In fact, this is the country's largest single military endeavor since the Korean conflict. And last week, as the Red crept ever closer to Winnipeg, all of the marshalled forces battled frantically to keep the rising waters out of the capital. "It's a war," said Lt.-Col. Steve Gillies of the Royal Canadian Horse Artillery as he directed the work of 600 troops under his command southwest of the city. "The enemy is at the gates. We cannot let him enter."

By Saturday evening, that mission was largely accomplished. As the Red's crest finally rolled into Winnipeg late last Thursday,

---

[6] Article by Barry Came, Dale Eisler, Jake MacDonald and Jane Stewart, from *Maclean's* 110:14-23 My 12 '97. Copyright © 1997 *Maclean's*. Reprinted with permission.

May 1, the city's defences creaked a little, springing an isolated leak or two, but in the end they held. The already swollen river rose a foot Thursday night, climbing to 24.4 feet above the winter ice level, enough to barely brush some of the city's bridges. Not enough, however, to spill over the city's 200 km of primary diking, a 26.5-foot-high system of raised riverside roads, parks, embankments and railroad tracks. "Today is looking good," breathed a relieved Winnipeg Mayor Susan Thompson as she arrived in her office on Friday morning. "What happened in the past 24 hours is a pretty positive development."

For that narrow escape, the city's 650,000 residents owe a large vote of thanks to the Red River Floodway. Completed in 1968, the 47-km-long water diversion was widely derided as "Duff's Ditch" when former Manitoba Premier Duff Roblin authorized its construction. But last week, as the Red's crest was moving 75,000 cubic feet of water every second through the heart of the city, the Floodway sent another 60,000 cubic feet per second coursing east of the city. To be sure, there were worries expressed by residents north of Winnipeg as they watched the Red's waters boil furiously out of the Floodway's exit, increasing the odds of severe flooding on the city's northern fringes. Their concerns echoed the complaints of flood victims south of the city in such unprotected communities as Ste. Agathe and Grande Pointe, where some residents felt they had been abandoned to save Winnipeg. "There's no doubt in my mind we're being sacrificed," said Grande Pointe resident Claude Lemoine, exhausted after a night of futile dike construction. But there could be no doubt that Duff's once notorious ditch played the key role in saving Manitoba's capital from untold damage.

"The Red's crest was moving 75,000 cubic feet of water every second through the heart of the city."

Despite the reprieve, the danger has not yet completely passed. "We've still got another week of white-knuckle time," Manitoba Premier Gary Filmon, a hydraulic engineer himself, told *Maclean's*. The peril lies in several directions. In the first place, the Red's high water is not going to ebb for some time. "That crest is going to stay up there for the next four or five days," cautioned Larry Whitney, Manitoba's chief flood liaison officer, on May 2. Even when it does finally move on, elevated water levels will likely persist in Winnipeg for at least two or three more weeks, all the time eating away at the city's extensive network of dikes.

Especially vulnerable are the secondary dikes that have been hastily constructed inside the fortified ring road all over the city by hordes of civilian volunteers, often working around the clock, and in the past few days by soldiers drawn from units right across the country. Most of these are slapdash affairs, fashioned from the Red River Valley's viscous mud and reinforced with roughly eight million sandbags—so ubiquitous a sight that local residents have now taken to labelling the sand-filled white plastic sacks "Red River perogies." Noted Winnipeg's chief flood engineer Doug McNeil: "All sandbagged dikes leak at some point, and the longer the river remains high, the greater the chances of a leak."

To counter the threat, the city has formed two shifts of 35 teams to continually monitor the secondary dikes. But there have already been dozens of leaks in the system. On the day the Red's crest rolled into Winnipeg, there were nine complete failures, resulting in the evacuation of dozens of families from threatened homes, including three apartment buildings in the downtown core.

Outside of Winnipeg, there is another potential peril lying to the southwest along the newly built Brunkild dike, sometimes called the Z dike for its zigzagging 40-km route, from the point where the Red enters Winnipeg to the tiny hamlet of Brunkild. The dike, an eight-metre-high wall of mud and crushed rock, was hastily erected in the past three weeks to prevent the Red from making an end run around Winnipeg's southern defences. Manitoba authorities feared the river's crest might swing west once it ran into the Winnipeg choke point, flowing first into the La Salle River, then coursing down the La Salle Valley to inundate the capital from the west. By itself, the Brunkild dike is an impressive sight. "It's a bloody engineering marvel that I think people around here are going to remember for a long time," said Gillies of the Horse Artillery as his troops struggled in bitterly cold 40 km/h winds, spiking erosion-resistant plastic sheeting along the dike's entire length.

By the end of last week, the Red's bulging crest, two metres deep in places, was lapping at the foot of the Brunkild dike. But the worst is yet to come. Provincial water resources engineers expect high water to hit the dike early this week, when forecast rainfall and southerly winds, gusting up to 40 km, could exacerbate the situation. One—or several—major breaches in the barrier might well spell trouble for Winnipeg's southern suburbs, especially the 4,200 residents of the bedroom community of St. Norbert.

Lying just beyond the perimeter highway that rings Winnipeg and is itself a primary dike, St. Norbert sits directly in the path of any floodwater that would flow from a breach in the Brunkild dike. To protect residents from that possibility, Manitoba's authorities ordered the complete evacuation of the community last Tuesday. Early that morning, as police and soldiers set up roadblocks to oversee the pullout, volunteers applied last-minute touches to a sandbagged dike around St. Norbert church, the same church where Father N. J. Ritchot and Louis Riel met on the night of Oct. 21, 1869, to launch the rebellion that led eventually to the founding of Manitoba. A few blocks away, Riel's great-grandnephew Joseph Riel, his wife, Joanne, and his mother, Marie, were packing up their belongings. "Last week, we volunteered to help out in St. Adolphe," said Joseph, a 37-year-old salesman. "We never dreamed that pretty soon they'd be volunteering to help us." His mother, pointing out that the family has been fighting Red River flooding for many generations, added: "But there had been nothing of the magnitude of this flood. When you see what happened in Ste. Agathe, it just gives you a chill."

Ste. Agathe, 24 km due south of Winnipeg, met its fate in the early hours of Tuesday morning. The town of 500, which sits on the west bank of the Red, was protected by a dike running along the river's edge. But it was overcome by a wall of water that rushed in from the opposite direction. Propelled by strong winds from the northwest, the flood washed over a highway and an elevated set of railway tracks west of the community. "Essentially, the water came in the backdoor," said flood liaison officer Whitney. Ste. Agathe postmaster Jean Champagne, the last civilian to flee the town, recalled: "A big, massive body of water came jumping over the west side of the highway. You could feel it coming. It was gushing, just like when you hear running rapids."

"Despite the gravity of the situation...there was a curious, almost festive, current running through all the preparations, aided by the outpouring of support...from the rest of the country."

Comments like that added urgency to the efforts then under way in Winnipeg and elsewhere in the province. Despite the gravity of the situation, however, there was a curious, almost festive, current running through all the preparations, aided by the outpouring of support—material as well as emotional—from the rest of the country. At the Brunkild dike, Gillies' troops, drawn from units scattered across the country, seemed to be enjoying the entire affair. Not far away, in the hockey arena at Sanford where the Horse Artillery's 2nd Regiment, based in Petawawa, Ont., was bivouacked, Bombardier Rob Morningstar, a 29-year-old native of St. Catharines, Ont., interrupted a lunch break to compare duty in Manitoba to that in war-torn Bosnia. "It's safer here and the food's a lot better," he commented. "It's also nice to do something for a change that might help to clean up the military's image in this country—you know, Somalia and all that stuff."

Much the same kind of spirit seemed to prevail in Winnipeg, where whole battalions of civilians daily volunteered for sandbag duty. "Sandbagging at school wasn't as much fun as at Kingston Crescent," said 12-year-old Jenneke Luit, a Grade 7 student at Westgate Mennonite Collegiate, not far from The Forks, where the Assiniboine River meets the Red in the heart of the city. "It was snowing, we were in the mud, and we ended up about two feet from the river that someone said has every disease known to man in it," the girl continued. "Kids were throwing sandbags in the mud on purpose. I had mud in my hair, caked in. And the worms were coming out, getting frozen."

Dan Donahue, a Kingston Crescent resident, remembered the moment the volunteers, including young Jenneke, turned up. "It's a very emotional thing, especially those first moments when the first group of 100 or so people arrive at your door and start sandbagging," said the music producer. "It's pretty phenomenal. At first, you feel, 'Oh, my nice quiet neighborhood is overrun.' And then, when they're all gone, you find that you miss them."

But if there have been lighter moments in the fight to rein in the Red, there have also been frayed nerves and anxious moments, particularly in the days leading up to the arrival of the river's crest. "There is no relief from the stress," Premier Filmon tells a visitor in his office on the second floor at the provincial legislature. He does not look any worse for wear, but he confesses all the same that his background—a master's degree in hydraulics and water resource management—is a mixed blessing. "It may be detrimental to have some technical knowledge," the premier remarks. "I'm not a worrier by nature, but I've seen the consequences of a burst dam and I've often gotten up lately with a huge lump in my stomach. Even though I'm relying on an army of people working co-operatively together to meet this challenge, I still have this sense that I'm ultimately responsible and that's a pretty scary thought."

Even if the river's power continues to be held in check, dealing with the aftermath is certain to be a daunting task. There are, as yet, no accurate estimates of the cost of the damage inflicted upon Manitoba. The bill, however, is likely to amount to several times the $25 million that Foreign Affairs Minister Lloyd Axworthy passed on to Filmon last week as a kind of down payment in advance of the final tally.

In the meantime, Canadians across the country have been opening their wallets, as well as their cupboards, to aid Manitoba's beleaguered flood victims. The Red Cross said Friday that it wants to raise $10 million through the Manitoba Food Appeal. Dozens of corporations have already donated, pushing the fund to $500,000 after three days. And on Friday morning, the besieged citizens of Winnipeg donated $15,000 in just one hour in a telethon. "The fund-raising is going great," said Red Cross spokesman Guy Tessier in Winnipeg. "We have raised about $500,000 in just one week." The major banks are all accepting donations, and the amount of money flowing in has been startling. By week's end, the Royal Bank, in conjunction with *Maclean's*, Rogers Multi-Media Inc. and CanWest Global, had taken in $150,000; Scotiabank, $43,000, and Toronto-Dominion Bank another $21,000. The Red Cross, meanwhile, had received $465,000 in pledges from across the country.

Aid has been coming in all shapes and forms. The Toronto Blue Jays baseball team collected money, as did the Calgary Philharmonic orchestra. In British Columbia, the Penticton Rotary Club is sending bottled water donated by a Vancouver company. Residents of the Saguenay River Valley in Quebec, with memories of last summer's disastrous floods fresh in their collective memory, raised $100,000. The CBC's Peter Gzowski staged a nationwide charity benefit on *Morningside*.

The public response has been so overwhelming that Gillies, for one, claimed to detect what he described as a "dawning sense of a patriotism" arising out of the "battle against a common foe." That may well be true. But if it is, there are those who have paid

"The Red Cross... wants to raise $10 million through the Manitoba Food Appeal."

a terrible price for the development. They are people like Red River farmer Ron Isaac, whose home and livelihood currently lie at the bottom of a shallow, muddy sea. "It's a very, very hard thing to bear," he mutters as he sits in his red pickup, staring across the churning water towards the trees that mark all that remains of what was once a flourishing farm and business. Thousands of Manitobans share his plight.

The Function of Hope[7]

It's not hard to understand why hope was one of the seven cardinal virtues of the medieval Catholic church. Hope, faith, and charity were the three "theological" virtues; courage (fortitude), temperance, justice, and prudence were the four "natural" virtues, derived from Aristotle. Makes an interesting list for organizations, doesn't it? Without hope, it's difficult to explain existence and impossible to imagine a future. How, without hope, can you explain school to a child or the entailments of teenage pregnancy to a young woman? How, without hope, can we in organizations expect commitment or creativity or community?

What is the organizational function of hope?

Over the years I can't recall reading in any management or leadership books anything about the organizational function of hope. You might define hope as an optimistic sense of the future, but it is also one of the most functional realities of society. A researcher interviewed on National Public Radio not too long ago talked about teenage pregnancy and called a "sense of the future" the best contraceptive. It's a wonderful way to think about hope.

"A lack of hope is utterly dismal and degrading and destructive to us personally, to us as a society."

A lack of hope is utterly dismal and degrading and destructive to us personally, to us as a society. American society is rapidly realigning itself into the hopeful and the hopeless, and tragically the hopeless group is growing far more rapidly than the hopeful group. We often suffer under an enormous national myth that because so many of us are doing well, we are a well society. I wish that were true, but of course it isn't. The belief that any of us can live without hope and still be healthy is a terrible deception. In a blind and single-minded defense of individual liberties we ignore the simple fact that when a sizable minority of the members of a body is ill, the entire body is ill.

Well, what can organizations ask about the function of hope? We can begin by asking the question, Of what is hope composed? Certainly part of the answer is the ability to make choices. To be without choices is a great tragedy, a tragedy leading to hopelessness or cynicism. The ability to make choices leads to other consequences. What do we choose? How do we choose? Our choices after all set us apart and shape our legacy.

The words *volition* and *volunteer* are rooted in the Latin word *velle*, which means "to wish" or "to choose." So even the dictionary tells us that choosing and doing what we wish are related. Perhaps that's why volunteers are usually enthusiastic: they have made a choice to do something they want to do. It's no mystery why so many nonprofit organizations are filled with enthusiastic people.

Neither is it strange to think of nonprofit work and choices as related. What else does Habitat for Humanity provide—along with a new house for people who otherwise could not afford one—than choice? Doesn't Doctors Without Borders supply entire lifetimes of choice along with medical care? As a way of building hope, nonprofit organizations create choices where none existed before.

Nonprofit groups themselves must make choices. Their choices are part of personal and organizational accountability to themselves and the people they serve. Thinking of choices, of course, is another way of looking at the stands we take, the friends and enemies we keep. Our choices guide our journey. Choices are part of our stewardship of life: What shall we promise? What do we owe? What may I keep? What must I abandon? No one said choices are easy.

Making the right choices requires competence, for many choices are risky. For years a man I knew at Herman Miller had worked at the same machine, doing the same job. For thirty-five years he invariably had a cold fried-egg sandwich on white bread for lunch. I once asked him why he didn't try something else. He told me that he liked the predictability of his fried-egg sandwich and that he hated making choices. I suppose if he had been forced to eat the same thing every day, he would have felt differently about it.

Another peculiar thing about choices, we are always making them whether we do so consciously or not. It seems to me that this is one reason so many people seek out volunteer organizations: places of realized potential guide us in the choices we make, guide us to hopeful and constructive choices that contribute to a common good. People who contribute to places of realized potential have chosen to give up self-centeredness for a larger goal, for a far higher calling than individual license. If you have chosen to join a nonprofit organization and if you choose to make that group a place of realized potential, you have made the choices that are possibly the only hope for our society.

Over many years of practice and reflection I have come to see that for organizations and society in general to be civil and healthy—two wonderful criteria—leaders provide for four primary needs and rights: opportunity, identity, and equity and the design of the task.

Any hopeful person has the opportunity to work, to be involved, to be needed. Isn't it my basic right in organizations to have the opportunity to share in work, to move continually toward my potential, the opportunity to be an owner—not necessarily of equipment and property but of ideas, process, community? Challenging work adds a meaning to our lives available from nowhere else.

Identity means inclusion. If I know who I am, I know where someone has to take me in—I know where home is. Identity means to know and to be known. Identity means to be respected. Identity means to be heard. Identity means the chance to be chosen. Identity means I have a name and a place.

Some time ago I got a note from a woman who works in the finishing department of one of Herman Miller's plants and who happens to be a friend of mine. She wrote me a wonderful letter about one of the company programs that she had been through and that she thought had special value. Then came the really important part of the letter. She invited me (I happened to be chairman of the board at the time) and the board of directors to attend the next session. Her belief that to invite the board of directors to a learning session was appropriate—as it surely was—reveals a strong sense of identity.

Equity means to be fairly treated. Equity means to have access. For many years we in the United States have talked about certain gifts—the gift of talent, the gift of health, the gift of wealth. The thing we see today is that the gift of access is more important than we ever realized—access to health care, access to education, access to influence, access to justice, access to mentors who care about our future.

Equity means to be seen as authentic—not because someone works in a certain department or because of a position or promotion. We are authentic before we acquire attributes, superficial and transitory characteristics, like these. Our jobs, our organizations, our work—these are certainly important, but we have to be seen as being authentic human beings no matter what *from the beginning*. To have true equity in a community or an organization means that we are legitimate there. Equity is an essential ingredient of hope.

Designing the task is the fourth job for leaders if they are to build hope in organizations. Since nonprofits are so various in their modes of operation, the job of designing the task will involve various people, but the job has to be done. Let me propose a series of questions that seem to me to lead to well-designed tasks.

> What is the unmet need or challenge facing the organization and its members? Why do we exist?

> How does what we do allow both individuals and the organization to express their potential? We do not work in a vacuum; neither should we labor unrewarded.

> Is the task clear for individuals and the organization? Clearly communicated? What will be measured? And when? Unmeasured work is like an unseen painting.

> Is the design of tasks both road map and treasure map? Does it give both clear direction and room for creative contributions? A well-designed task requires more than a manual.

"The thing we see today is that the gift of access is more important than we ever realized [including] access to mentors who care about our future."

> Does the design of the task allow each member of the
> group to answer the question, What is *my* role? How
> are we connected with the group's effort to serve a
> larger good?

Work in nonprofits often moves easily to competence without becoming diverted by position. I have often asked myself why this is. The answer seems to come from the nature of the group— a movement enlists followers rather than pressing them into positions, titles, and roles. Designing the task for a movement means exposing what needs to be done, not imposing assignments on draftees. Designing the task means asking the question, How can you contribute? Then of course we must listen carefully to the answer. And in the end, designing the task means laying the foundation for hope.

"Individual liberty, highly prized in American society, exists always in relation to a common good."

I believe that hope can be thought of in terms of the obligations of leadership. Hope encourages maturity and continuity and accountability. Sadly a dearth of hope may be the most serious long-term reality in our society today. The nature of hope, of its organizational and societal role, requires us to see community as an essential condition for all. Individual liberty, highly prized in American society, exists always in relation to a common good.

In our families, in our organizations, in our society, who's going to be remembered for the gift of hope? How can each one of us become responsible for creating hope?

It seems to me that nonprofit groups are infinitely more adept at building hope than other kinds of organizations are. Through their vision, their commitment to service, their convictions concerning the common good, they have earned a distinctive position as builders of hope. Among the dozens of nonprofits each of us knows generally or in some cases intimately are models of hope-giving we can emulate. We know the local school board, the hospital, the scout troop. By their existence and their work, they give us hope for the future of our own organizational lives.

Perhaps of all the virtues hope is the most fragile, the most fleeting, the least concrete. Don't forget that the Greek gods, at the very bottom of Pandora's box of ills and troubles, placed hope. Hope it is that allows us to cope with the rest of life. Nonprofit organizations more than any other groups in our world build hope, restore hope, exemplify hope. Nonprofit groups begin by building hope for the world and thereby build it for themselves. How can we quantify the hope created by the Peace Corps or the Red Cross or the Salvation Army? After all the money has been spent, the classes taught, the help given, the medicines distributed—isn't it hope that remains and grows?

Bibliography

An asterisk (*) preceding a reference indicates that an excerpt from the work has been reprinted in this compilation or that the work has been cited.

Books and Pamphlets

Boyte, Harry Chatten and Nancy N. Kari. *Building America: The Democratic Promise of Public Work*. Philadelphia: Temple University Press, 1996.

Brainerd, Wesley and Ed Malles, eds. *Bridge Building in Wartime: Colonel Wesley Brainerd's Memoir of the 50th New York Volunteer Engineers*. Knoxville: University of Tennessee Press, 1997.

Cowart, John. *The Prison Minister's Handbook: Volunteer Ministry to the Forgotten Christian*. San Jose: Resource, 1996.

*De Pree, Max. *Leading Without Power: Finding Hope in Serving Community*. San Francisco: Jossey-Bass Inc., 1997.

Dickens, Monica and Carlton Jackson, eds. *Befriending: The American Samaritans*. Bowling Green, OH: Bowling Green State University Popular Press, 1996.

Ellis, Susan J. *The Volunteer Recruitment and Membership Development Book*. Philadelphia: Energize Assocs., 1996.

Ellis, Susan J.; Jeffrey D. Kahn and Alan S. Glazer. *From the Top Down: The Executive Role in Volunteer Program Success*. Philadelphia: Energize Assocs., 1996.

Jackson, Vera R., ed. *Volunteerism in Geriatric Settings*. Binghamton, NY: Haworth Press, 1996.

*Jacoby, Barbara, and associates. *Service-Learning in Higher Education: Concepts and Practices*. San Francisco: Jossey-Bass Inc., 1996.

Kilpatrick, Joseph and Sanford Danziger, compilers. *Better Than Money Can Buy: The New Volunteers*. Winston-Salem, NC: Innersearch Pub., 1996.

Kipps, Harriet Clyde, ed. *Volunteer America: A Comprehensive National Guide to Opportunities for Service, Training, and Work Experience*. Chicago: J. G. Ferguson, 1997.

Lowenthal, Phil; Stephanie Tarnoff and Lisa David, eds. *Alternatives to the Peace Corps: A Directory of Third World and U.S. Volunteer Opportunities*. Oakland: Food First, 1996.

Munton, Don, ed. *Siting by Choice: Waste Facilities, NIMBY, and Volunteer Communities*. Washington, DC: Georgetown University Press, 1996.

Perkins, Kenneth B. and John Benoit. *The Future of Volunteer Fire and Rescue Services: Taming the Dragons of Change*. Stillwater, OK: IFSTA/ Fire Protection, 1996.

Rodeman, Steve; Jim Jerving, producer; and Laura Beaudoin, ed. *Volunteer Leadership Program: A Director's Guide to Credit Union Regulations and Exams VL11*. Dubuque, IA: Kendall/Hunt, 1997.

Scanlon, Thomas J. *Waiting for the Snow: The Peace Corps Papers of a Charter Volunteer*. Chevy Chase, MD: Posterity Press, 1997.

Schreck, Harley Carl. *The Elderly in America: Volunteerism and Neighborhood in Seattle*. Lanham, MD: University Press of America, 1996.

Waldman, Steven. *The Bill: How the Adventures of Clinton's National Service Bill Reveal What Is Corrupt, Comic, Cynical, and Noble About Washington*. New York: Viking Books, 1995.

Walker, Alan and Lorna Warren. *Changing Services for Older People: The Neighbourhood Support Units Innovation*. Bristol, PA: Open University Press, 1996.

Additional Periodical Articles with Abstracts

For those who wish to read more widely on the subject of volunteerism, this section contains abstracts of additional articles that bear on the topic. Readers who require a comprehensive list of materials are advised to consult *Readers' Guide Abstracts* and other Wilson indexes.

Corporate Assets. Carole Schweitzer. *Association Management* 50:30-3 + Ja '98

Barbara Lohman, spokesperson for the Points of Light Foundation in Washington, D.C., maintains that plenty of evidence exists to prove that corporate CEOs are employing their organizations' assets—both financial and human—as management tools that can be applied to nonprofit leadership. According to three corporate CEOs whose leadership roles as volunteer leaders of associations provide perspectives on both volunteerism and corporate profitability, business and association leadership are developing more similarities than differences. All three find that they are adopting management skills and leadership styles from the crucible of corporate experience to successfully influence the nonprofit agenda. In addition, they have found that the nonprofit organization has a lesson or two to offer in return. The views of these three CEOs—experienced volunteer leaders J. Michael Cook, Phyllis Campbell, and Shirley DeLibero—are discussed.

How the New Law Will Affect Associations. Jerald A. Jacobs. *Association Management* 49:39-41 Ag '97

Part of a special section on the Volunteer Protection Act of 1997. The new, federal Volunteer Protection Act of 1997 offers immunity from personal liability to those who volunteer for nonprofit organizations. The act is designed to encourage volunteerism and facilitate volunteer organization recruiting by decreasing the legal liability risks to individuals who decide to volunteer. The law preempts inconsistent state laws and standardizes protection that currently varies significantly from state to state. The law is complex, containing many conditions, qualifications, and restrictions. In addition, due to the fact that no federal agency is authorized to interpret the law, clarification will likely have to await court determinations on a case-by-case basis where claimants try to hold volunteers personally responsible and the law is used as a defense on behalf of the volunteers. Some of the practical considerations regarding the law's impact on associations are examined.

All for a Good Cause. Jennifer Low. *Canadian Banker* 104:21-6 Ja/F '97

When there is an opportunity to assist others in their local communities, Canadian banks and bankers not only contribute money but also give generously of their time, expertise, and enthusiasm. The major banks have developed creative new strategies toward community work. Today, a roll-up-the-sleeves approach to volunteerism is sweeping through banks throughout the nation, with much of it starting at the branch level. Supporting a cause is the key to creating a strong corporate presence in a community. Some bankers think that this burst of community activity is a natural extension of the rise of relationship banking. Another explanation provided by bankers is that budgets are diminishing while the number of requests for support from charities and nonprofit groups continues to rise. As a result, banks must be more inventive about the solutions that they provide in order to help needy groups while building goodwill within the community. Managers concur that although community work does not necessarily have a bottom-line reward, it always increases employee morale. The volunteer activities of Ron Lambert, area manager for National Bank of Canada, and of employees at the following banks are described: Royal Bank, Bank of Montreal, CIBC, Toronto Dominion Bank, and Scotiabank.

Hospital Volunteerism in the '90s. Elizabeth S. Pforzheimer and Ann R. Miller. *Hospitals and Health Networks* 70:80 F 20 '96

In order to appropriately recruit, train, and make best use of their volunteers' time, it is crucial that hospitals get to know their volunteers. Increasingly, volunteers are professionals seeking a kind of fulfillment that is not provided by their high-pressure jobs. Most likely, these people have limited time—often evenings and weekends—but believe strongly in giving to their communities. Although volunteers continue to perform the customary roles of gift shop operator, desk greeter, and benefit chair, many are using their professional skills and undertaking important responsibilities to extend the capabilities of the hospital staff. The responsibilities of hospitals in this new environment are discussed.

Operations That Build Smiles, Confidence, Skills and Community Goodwill. Martha I. Finney. *HRMagazine* 42:110-12 + Ap '97

Employees are increasingly acting on their desire to get involved in volunteer and charitable activities. According to a Gallup survey sponsored by the Independent Sector, a Washington-based association of nonprofit organizations, a record 93 million Americans did some form of volunteer work during 1995. Another survey of 250,000 college freshmen, sponsored by UCLA's Higher Education Research Institute, showed that a record 72 percent served in a volunteer capacity during 1996. Citibank employee Ed Dixon's involvement with Operation Smile, a Norfolk, Virginia-based nonprofit volunteer organization in which surgeons spend their own vacation time repairing the facial deformities of children in impoverished countries, is discussed; the effect that a volunteer culture can have on recruiting and sales is outlined; the rewards that getting involved in a volunteer program can present to individuals are examined; and the benefits that supporting community involvement and employee volunteerism can present to organizations, as well as ways in which companies can support such activities, are highlighted.

A Volunteer Leader with Heart. Bill Leonard. *HRMagazine* 43:98-100 + Ja '98

A profile of Kathleen McComber, the first Arkansan to be elected chair of the Society for Human Resource Management (SHRM) board of directors. McComber maintains that her involvement as a volunteer leader with SHRM arises from the need to support and give back something to the human resources (HR) profession—a profession in which she has excelled. Her strong feelings about the importance of volunteering have resulted in her making "volunteerism" the theme for her year as SHRM board chair. A core element of her volunteerism theme is what McComber calls "The Have A HEART Campaign." The acronym, H-E-A-R-T (Help Everyone Achieve Respect Today), spells out the central tenet of the campaign. McComber says that she wants to focus on volunteering through the HR profession in some way. She considers school-to-work and community education programs to be excellent ways for HR professionals to become involved. McComber's career details are presented.

Volunteerism: Community Service or Involuntary Servitude? Jesse L. Jackson, Jr. *Journal of Housing and Community Development* 54:12-14 N/D '97

The Housing Opportunity and Responsibility Act of 1997 (HR 2), which is working its way through Congress, would mandate that public and assisted housing residents volunteer to perform eight hours of community service every month in order to maintain their eligibility for housing subsidies. Middle- and upper-class recipients of housing subsidies in the form of income-tax deductions for mortgage interest payments do not have to volunteer their time in exchange for the benefits that they receive, and they do not risk eviction for noncompliance, as public housing residents who do not volunteer do. If approved, the measure would require mandatory work without compensation and would have the unintended impact of displacing thousands of low-wage employees who are making the transition from welfare to work.

Step Up to Learning with PREP. Mary L. Noyd and Bertha Richardson. *Journal of Staff Development* 17:18-19 Spring '96

Part of a special issue on staff development for character development. The introduction of the Personal Responsibility Education Process (PREP) in the School District of University City, Missouri, is discussed. A curriculum integration team of teachers involved in character education was organized to develop skills that would assist other teachers in the district in infusing PREP into the curriculum. The team decided on the ten character traits of respect, responsibility, belonging, self-esteem, cooperation, loyalty, honesty, unselfishness, perseverance, and volunteerism, which would be used throughout the district. The team initiated the program with motivational materials for the beginning of the school year. Ongoing staff development has been used to implement the program, and members of the curriculum integration team provide on-site training in each school.

The Key to Successful School to Work Programs for Blind or Visually Impaired Students. Karen E. Wolffe. *Journal of Visual Impairment and Blindness* 91:5-7 Jl/Ag '97

The most successful school-to-work programs for blind or visually impaired students share some basic components. These components are paid work, collaboration, job-readiness training, self-initiated job searches, connections to the future, diversity, goals, limited use of supports, evaluation, self-advocacy and volunteerism, and enthusiasm.

Making the Possible Real. Mary E. Tracy. *Momentum* 28:7-9 O/N '97

Part of a special section on institutional advancement. Well-designed, successful advancement programs contain the three elements of strong and involved leadership, challenging financial goals and strategies, and volunteerism. Successful school leaders inspire increasing numbers of the school's constituents to invest in the institutional mission. To this end, schools are revising their leadership structures to accommodate the position of president with responsibility for mission articulation and resource development. There must be broad involvement from outside and within the school in advancing the school's fund-raising strategies, which include the annual fund, capital campaign, major gifts, and planned giving. Volunteers are also an essential part of an advancement program, and there is a noteworthy connection between people's volunteer involvement and their decision to give a gift.

Service: A Tradition. Patrice Hughes. *Momentum* 28:58 Ag/S '97

Part of a special section on Catholic social teaching. The effect and range of the Catholic educational community's efforts promote Catholic social teaching and support the goal of the Presidents' Summit for America's Future. The summit, which was held in Philadelphia in spring 1997, focused on volunteerism, which is a traditional practice in Catholic education.

The Culture of Renewal: Characteristics of the Community Renewal Movement. Richard Louv. *National Civic Review* 85:52-61 Winter '96

Part of a special issue on the role of nonprofit organizations in renewing community. In the first of a two-part article on signs of community renewal underway across the U.S., the writer explores how renewal can be seen in neighborhoods, communications, workplaces, and charitable contributions throughout the country. He examines the new language of community; the way in which the culture of renewal is reviving neighborhoods; the exciting "architecture of renewal" that is emerging; the 21st-century tools that will be employed in the culture of renewal; the way in which the culture of renewal is nurturing a new business ethic; and the new rules of charity and volunteerism that are being created by the culture of renewal.

The Limits of Charity Daniel Schorr. *New Leader* 80:4-5 Ap 21 '97

If volunteerism is to work where the need is greatest, the inner city, it will have to be more than just feel-good sentiment. General Colin L. Powell, presiding over the Philadelphia summit on volunteerism, said it was all about getting Americans off the sidelines and into the game. Youth mentoring, which could be one of the most effective and useful of services, needs volunteers, however. Mentoring is not an activity for occasional spare-time hours, moreover, and in order to have a positive effect mentors need supporting structures. As Nicholas Lemann argued in Newsweek, any serious campaign to save America's children would need the support of Washington's money and strength.

This Way to the Active Community. Alun Michael. *New Statesman* 127:20-1 F 20 '98

The writer discusses the relationship between the British Labour Party government and volunteerism. He argues that voluntary and community activity is a powerful means of social inclusion and of enabling everyone, no matter what their background, skills, race, or age, to make a positive contribution to an active community. He states that voluntary and community action is the personal response of individuals to social need and that the role of government is not to control such action but to create a climate in which it can flourish. He contends that the voluntary sector needs a sympathetic government, just as the government needs a healthy, innovative, and creative voluntary sector that is fully conscious of its independence but willing to work in partnership. He suggests that the private sector must also be involved and that there should be a triangular relationship that allows voluntary organizations, business, and government to share their strengths and expertise.

Virginia's Free-Market Environmentalist. Gregory A. Fossedal and John Shanahan. *Policy Review* 87:12-14 Ja/F '98

Becky Norton Dunlop is a controversial but highly successful figure in environmental circles in Virginia. During her term as head of the secretariat for environmental protection and natural resources, she created a highly successful model of how a state can encourage environmental concerns without sacrificing freedom or economic growth. Dunlop developed a system of environmental protection that achieved cleaner air, cleaner water, a reduction in the number of hazardous sites, more volunteerism in parks, and a better relationship between business and state regulators. Her approach, which relies heavily on cooperation, has earned the anger of the green movement. Moreover, she is such a controversial figure that James Gilmore, the Republican governor-elect of Virginia, promised that he would not reappoint her if he were elected. Dunlop's career is discussed.

Reading, Writing...and Wedding Receptions. C. L. Taylor. *Principal* 76:18-21 N '96

Part of a special section on principals, school, and community. At a time when local government budgets are shrinking, school districts throughout the U.S. are finding that the demand for community use of school buildings and grounds is higher than ever. Many administrators agree that welcoming the community into the school has a positive effect on students, the most direct benefits being increased volunteerism and the involvement of families and neighborhood residents. Another important benefit is greater community support when school systems seek funds to build new and improved facilities. Many administrators view community use of schools as an opportunity rather than a challenge.

Measuring the Outcomes of Community-wide Study Circle Programs. Matt Leighninger. *Public Management* 78:39-41 S '96

Measuring the outcomes of a new kind of citizen involvement project called the community-wide study circle program is discussed. Study circles are small, democratic, and highly participatory discussion groups, which are intended to stimulate dialogue, create new action opportunities, and generate volunteerism in the community. Due to their nature and make-up, it would be a mistake to look at study circles only in the context of the specific outcomes that they produce. By uncovering new leaders in the community, forging new connections, and reinvigorating existing institutions, study circles provide the foundation for more effective, community-based problem solving. Moreover, as community members gain opportunities to create their own results, the outcomes of these programs fit into the local context and are more likely to receive broad local support.

Capital Cynics. Virginia I. Postrel. *Reason* 29:4+ Ag/S '97

An attitude of resigned cynicism toward Washington is brewing. Washington's persistent camera hogging, sound biting, and story manufacturing is both cynical and condescending. By treating Americans as simpering fools, Washington's constant spinning contaminates everything it touches, but people are too media-aware to be so simply duped. Last May's "volunteerism" summit was a cynical corruption of the work of millions of volunteers and was designed to focus the cameras on the me-me-me of Washington talking heads and politicians. The cynicism that greeted the summit from journalists and many conservative commentators was a suitable response to a fake public relations stunt. The good news is that Washington's annoying behavior is the natural result of its increasing irrelevance and of its being ignored.

Volunteerism as the Seedbed of Democracy: The Educational Thought and Practice of Guy Henson of Nova Scotia. Michael R. Welton and James Lecky. *Studies in the Education of Adults* 29:25-38 Ap '97

The writers discuss the educational thought and practice of Guy Henson of Nova Scotia in Canada, his concept of democracy and the place of adult education in the democratic state. Henson was the first director of the Adult Education Division for Nova Scotia from 1946 to 1956, having set up the division from a carefully planned theoretical and practical base. For Henson, adult education was closely connected to his vision of democracy, to community life and development, and to the development of individuals. Democracy depended on the self-worth of the populace, which was made up of intelligent and critically thinking individuals who would deal with topical and controversial issues and together would organize and develop their communities. He envisioned a mutually beneficial relationship between the state and volunteer agencies, whereby people would be given the means to get the best from the state without state dominance or interference. For Henson, vocational education went beyond mere skill acquisition and involved providing people with the means to ponder economic, social, and political issues.

The General's Next Campaign. Margaret B. Carlson. *Time* 149:28-9 Mr 17 '97

General Colin Powell will serve as general chairman of the Presidents' Summit for America's Future, an event promoting volunteerism. Since deciding not to run for president, Powell has had many offers from corporate boards, foundations, and academia. The challenge for Powell is not to attract offers, however, it is to separate the ideas that will work from those that will not. Although he earns big fees for giving speeches, Powell spends 30 percent of his time on the summit, and he expects that amount to increase. Before the launch of the project, Powell had already rescued volunteerism from its second-class status as women's work. Now, as politics declines even further, he has taken on the task of revitalizing civic life. If he succeeds, this will lead to increased calls for him to salvage politics as well.

Involuntary Volunteers. John Cloud. *Time* 150:76 D 1 '97

Public schools are beginning to require students to provide a service for their communities. Mandatory volunteerism has become the latest fad in public schools, and nationwide almost one-fifth of students surveyed in 1996 said they attend schools that mandate service. Proponents of the system claim it will help reconnect frayed communities by showing young citizens that they can make a difference. Mandatory volunteerism at Dunbar High in Baltimore, Maryland, is discussed.

A Damning Moment. Arianna Stassinopoulos Huffington. *U.S. News & World Report* 122:30 My 19 '97

The conservatives' argument that they do care about the poor but that nongovernmental means of helping them are more effective may turn out to be a sham. Modern conservatism is now caught in a damning moment, crystallized by the reactions to the president's volunteerism summit. Whatever its failings, the summit represented the type of thing conservatives are supposed to be for: It emphasized private-sector responses to social problems, no taxpayer money was spent, and not one legislative initiative was endorsed by the summiteers. Nonetheless, conservatives were apoplectic over the summit's ideals. Conservatives will never be able to cut the role of government until they have convinced the public that there are alternative ways of caring for those in need.

Powell Volunteers His Ideas on Helping. Julian E. Barnes and Michael J. Gerson. *U.S. News & World Report* 123:7 D 8 '97

Colin Powell has been reviewing efforts to put into action the goals of this year's volunteerism summit, but data are difficult to obtain. America's Promise, the summit's follow-on organization, received only a 70 percent response to requests for updates from all organizations that made pledges at the summit, as some big organizations were still collecting information on their efforts. Nonetheless, more than 41 cities and 13 states have held local follow-up summits, and around 81 are planned for the first half of 1998.

Appendix

Organizations

American Red Cross
(Many sites across the world.)
150 Amsterdam Ave
New York, NY 10023-5025
Ph: 212-787-1000
Fx: 212-875-2309
www.redcross.org

American Society of Directors of Volunteer Services
One North Franklin
31st Floor
Chicago, IL 60606
Ph: 312-422-3939
Fx: 312-422-4575
www.asdvs.org

AmeriCorps*VISTA (Volunteers in Service to America) 1-888-507-5962
www.libertynet.org/zelson/section1.html

Big Brothers/Big Sisters of America
230 North 13th Street
Philadelphia, PA 19107
Ph: 215-567-7000
www.bbbsa.org

Habitat for Humanity International
121 Habitat Street
Americus, GA 31709
Ph: (912) 924-6935
www.habitat.org

Impact Online, Inc.
325 "B" Forest Ave.
Palo Alto, CA 94301
Ph: 650-327-1389
Fx: 650-327-1395
E-mail: respond@impactonline.org
www.volunteermatch.org

Jesuit Volunteer Corps
PO Box 25478
Washington, DC 20007
Ph: 202-687-1132
www2.ari.net

New York Cares
116 E. 16th Street
New York, NY 10003
Ph: 212-228-5000
Fx: 212-228-6414
Email: ny_cares@nycares.com
www.ny.cares.org

Peace Corps
1990 K Street, NW
Washington, DC 20526
Ph: 1-800-424-8580
www.peacecorps.gov

Retired & Senior Volunteer Program (RSVP)
Mary L. Singleton Senior Center
150 E. First Street
Jacksonville, FL 32206
Ph: 904-630-0998
Fx: 904-630-0511

Senior Volunteer Advisory Services
1819 H Street N.W., Suite 660
Washington, DC 20006
Ph: 1-202-496-9671
Fx: 1-202-496-9673
E-mail: SVAS@mnsinc.com
www.svas.org

Volunteer Lawyer Program
Rhode Island Bar Association
115 Cedar Street
Providence, RI 02903
Ph: 401 421-5740
Fx: 401-421-2703
1-800-339-7758
www.ribar.com

Corporations for National Service: State Commissions

Alabama
950 22nd St., North, Ste. 428
Birmingham, AL 35203
(205) 731-0027
FAX: (205) 731-0031

Alaska
State Community Service Commission
915 Second Ave., Ste. 3190
Seattle, WA 98174-1103
(206) 220-7736
FAX: (206) 553-4415
http://www.comregaf.state.ak.us/ASCSC.htm

Arizona
522 North Central, Rm. 205A
Phoenix, AZ 85004-2190
(602) 379-4825
FAX: (602) 379-4030

Arkansas
700 West Capitol St., Rm. 2506
Little Rock, AR 72201
(501) 324-5234
FAX: (501) 324-6949

California
Commission on Improving Life Through
  Service
1100 Wilshire Blvd., Rm. 11221
Los Angeles, CA 90024
(310) 235-7421
FAX: (310) 235-7422
http://www.cilts.ca.gov

Colorado
Governor's Commission on National and
  Community Service
140 E. 19th Ave., Ste. 210
Denver, CO 80203-1167
(303) 866-1070
FAX: (303) 866-1081
http://home.earthlink.net/ ~ americorps/

Connecticut
Commission on National and Community
  Service
1 Commercial Plaza, 21st Floor
Hartford, CT 06103-3510
(203) 240-3237
FAX: (203) 240-3238
http://ctdhe.commnet.edu/dheweb/ameri.htm

Delaware and (MD)
One Market Center, Box 5
300 W. Lexington St., Ste. 702
Baltimore, MD 21201-3418
(410) 962-4443
FAX: (410) 962-3201

District of Columbia (and VA)
400 North 8th St.
P.O. Box 10066
Richmond, VA 23240-1832
(804) 771-2197
FAX: (804) 771-2157

Florida
Commission on Community Service
3165 McCrory St., Ste. 115
Orlando, FL 32803-3750
(407) 648-6117
FAX: (407) 648-6116
http://www.fccs.org/

Georgia
Commission on National and Community
  Service
75 Piedmont Ave., N.E. Ste. 462
Atlanta, GA 30303-2587
(404) 331-4646
FAX: (404) 331-2898
http://www.mindspring.com/ ~ gcncs

Hawaii
300 Ala Moana Blvd., Rm. 6326
Honolulu, HI 96850-0001
(808) 541-2832
FAX: (808) 3603

Idaho
304 North 8th St., Rm. 344
Boise, ID 83702-5835
(208) 334-1707
FAX: (208) 334-1421

Illinois
77 West Jackson Blvd., Ste. 442
Chicago, IL 60604-3511
(312) 353-3622
FAX: (312) 353-5343

Indiana
46 East Ohio St., Rm. 457
Indianapolis, IN 46204-1922
(317) 226-6724
FAX: (317) 226-5437

Iowa
210 Walnut St., Rm. 917
Des Moines, IA 50309-2195
(515) 284-4816
FAX: (515) 284-6640

Kansas
444 S.E. Quincy, Rm. 260
Topeka, KS 66683-3572
(785) 295-2540
FAX: (785) 295-2596

Kentucky
600 Martin Luther King Pl., Rm. 372-D
Louisville, KY 40202-2230
(502) 582-6384
FAX: (502) 582-6386

Louisiana
640 Main St., Ste. 102
Baton Rouge, LA 70801-1910
(504) 389-0471
FAX: (504) 389-0510

Maine (and NH & VT)
Commission for Community Service
91-93 North State St.
Concord, NH 03301-3939
(603) 225-1450
FAX: (603) 225-1459
http://www.state.me.us/spo/mccs/index.htm

Maryland (and DE)
Governor's Commission on Service
One Market Center, Box 5
300 W. Lexington St., Ste. 702
Baltimore, MD 21201-3418
(410) 962-4443
FAX: (410) 962-3201
http://www.mgcos.state.md.us/mgcos

Massachusetts
Service Alliance
10 Causeway St., Ste. 469
Boston, MA 02222-1038
(617) 565-7018
FAX: (617) 565-8607
http://www.msalliance.org/

Michigan
211 West Fort St., Ste. 1408
Detroit, MI 48226-2799
(313) 226-7848
FAX: (313) 226-2557

Minnesota
431 South 7th St., Rm. 2480
Minneapolis, MN 55415-1854
(612) 334-4083
FAX: (612) 334-4084

Mississippi
Commission for Volunteer Service
100 West Capital St., Rm. 1005A
Jackson, MS 39269-1092
(601) 965-5664
FAX: (601) 965-4617
http://www.mcvs.org/

Missouri
801 Walnut St., Ste. 504
Kansas City, MO 64106-2009
(816) 374-6300
FAX: (816) 374-6305

Montana
208 North Montana Ave., Ste. 206
Helena, MT 59601-3837
(406) 449-5404
FAX: (406) 449-5412

Nebraska
Commission for National and Community
  Service
100 Centennial Mall North, Rm. 156
Lincoln, NE 68508-3896
(402) 437-5493
FAX: (402) 437-5495
http://www.nol.org/home/NCNCS/

Nevada
4600 Kietzke Ln., Ste. E-141
Reno, NV 89502-5033
(702) 784-5314
(702) 784-5026

New Hampshire (and ME & VT)
Commission on National and Community
  Service
91-93 North State St.
Concord, NH 03301-3939
(603) 225-1450
FAX: (603) 225-1459
http://www.americorps.nh.com/

New Jersey
44 South Clinton Ave., Rm. 702
Trenton, NJ 08609-1507
(609) 989-2243
FAX: (609) 989-2304

New Mexico
120 S. Federal Pl., Ste. 315
Santa Fe, NM 87501-2026
(505) 988-6577
FAX: (505) 988-6661

New York
State Commission on National and
  Community Service
6 World Trade Center, Rm. 758
New York, NY 10048-0206
(212) 637-5010
FAX: (212) 466-4195
http://www.nyscncs.org

Leo O'Brien Federal Building, Rm. 818
Clinton Ave. & N. Pearl St.
Albany, NY 12207
(518) 431-4150

North Carolina
300 Fayetteville St. Mall, Rm. 131
Raleigh, NC 27601-1739
(919) 856-4731
FAX: (919) 856-4738

North Dakota (and SD)
225 S. Pierre St., Rm. 225
Pierre, SD 57501-2452
(605) 224-5996
FAX: (605) 224-9201

Ohio
Governor's Community Service Council
51 North High St., Ste. 451
Columbus, OH 43215
(614) 469-7441
FAX: (614) 469-2125
http://www.state.oh.us/ohiogcsc/

Oklahoma
215 Dean A. McGee, Ste. 324
Oklahoma City, OK 73102
(405) 231-5201
FAX: (405) 231-4329

Oregon
Commission for National and Community
  Service
2010 Lloyd Center
Portland, OR 97232
(503) 231-2103
FAX: (503) 231-2106
http://www.nwrel.org/edwork/americorps/ore-
gon/

Pennsylvania
3535 Market St., Rm. 2460
Philadelphia, PA
19104-2996
(215) 596-4077
FAX: (215) 596-4072

Rhode Island
400 Westminster St., Rm. 203
Providence, RI 02903
(401) 528-5424
FAX: (401) 528-5220

South Carolina
1835 Assembly St., Ste. 872
Columbia, SC 29201-2430
(803) 765-5771
FAX: (803) 765-5777

South Dakota (and ND)
225 S. Pierre St., Rm. 225
Pierre, SD 57501-5996
(605) 224-5996
FAX: (605) 224-9201

Tennessee
265 Cumberland Bend Dr.
Nashville, TN 37228
(615) 736-5561
FAX: (615) 736-7937

Texas
Commission for National and Community
  Service
903 San Jacinto, Ste. 130
Austin, TX 78701-3747
(512) 916-5671
FAX: (512) 916-5806
http://www.txcncs.state.tx.us/

Utah
350 South Main St., Rm. 504
Salt Lake City, UT
84101-2198
(801) 524-5411
FAX: (801) 524-3599

Vermont (and ME & NH)
Commission on National and Community
  Service
91-93 North State St.
Concord, NH 03301-3939
(603) 225-1450
FAX: (603) 225-1459
http://www.state.vt.us/cncs/

Virginia (and DC)
400 North 8th St.,
P.O. Box 10066
Richmond, VA 23240-1832
(804) 771-2197
FAX: (804) 771-2157

Washington
Commission on National and Community
  Service
915 Second Ave., Ste. 3190
Seattle, WA 98174-1103
(206) 220-7745
FAX: (206) 553-4415
http://www.wa.gov/wcncs

West Virginia
10 Hale St., Ste. 203
Charleston, WV
25301-1409
(304) 347-5246
FAX: (304) 347-5464

Wisconsin
310 W. Wisconsin Ave., Rm. 1240
Milwaukee, WI 53203-2211
(414) 297-1118
FAX: (414) 297-1863

Wyoming
2120 Capitol Ave., Rm. 1110
Cheyenne, WY
82001-3649
(307) 772-2385
FAX: (307) 772-2389

Index